# JUMPING INTO PLYOMETRICS

**Donald A. Chu, PhD**
**Ather Sports Injury Clinic**
**Castro Valley, California**

**Leisure Press**
Champaign, Illinois

**Library of Congress Cataloging-in-Publication Data**

Chu, Donald A. (Donald Allen), 1940-
    Jumping into plyometrics / Donald A. Chu.
        p.      cm.
    ISBN 0-88011-443-6
    1. Physical education and training.   2. Exercise.   I. Title.
    GV711.C54   1991
    613.7'11--dc20

90-28372
CIP

ISBN: 0-88011-443-6

0-87322-515-5 (book/video package—VHS)

0-87322-517-1 (book/video package—PAL)

Copyright © 1992 by Donald A. Chu

**Developmental Editor**: Holly Gilly; **Assistant Editor**: Elizabeth Bridgett; **Copyeditor**: Molly Bentsen; **Proofreader**: Dianna Matlosz; **Production Director**: Ernie Noa; **Typesetter**: Angela K. Snyder; **Text Design**: Keith Blomberg; **Text Layout**: Tara Welsch; **Cover Design**: Jack Davis; **Cover Photo**: Will Zehr; **Illustrations**: Keith Blomberg; **Printer**: United Graphics

Leisure Press books are available at special discounts for bulk purchase. Special editions or book excerpts can also be created to specification. For details, contact the Special Sales Manager at Human Kinetics.

Printed in the United States of America      10  9

**Leisure Press**
A Division of Human Kinetics
Web site: http://www.humankinetics.com

*United States:* Human Kinetics, P.O. Box 5076, Champaign, IL 61825-5076
1-800-747-4457
e-mail: humank@hkusa.com

*Canada:* Human Kinetics, Box 24040, Windsor, ON N8Y 4Y9
1-800-465-7301 (in Canada only)
e-mail: humank@hkcanada.com

*Europe:* Human Kinetics, P.O. Box IW14, Leeds LS16 6TR, United Kingdom
(44) 1132 781708
e-mail: humank@hkeurope.com

*Australia:* Human Kinetics, 57A Price Avenue, Lower Mitcham, South Australia 5062
(08) 277 1555
e-mail: humank@hkaustralia.com

*New Zealand:* Human Kinetics, P.O. Box 105-231, Auckland 1
(09) 523 3462
e-mail: humank@hknewz.com

# CONTENTS

# PREFACE

All athletes strive to be a little stronger, a little faster, knowing that this edge in ability leads them ever closer to realizing their ultimate potential.

The realization of highly held goals is a product of the development of natural ability and the learned skills or technique of a sport. The typical athlete must train for many years to refine technique and to develop the strength and speed required to reach his or her individual potential.

Plyometrics is exercise designed to enhance the athlete's ability to blend speed and strength training. It is, in effect, "the icing on the cake." When sound training principles are used, plyometrics offers the mechanism by which an athlete can start quicker, change direction more rapidly, accelerate faster, and improve overall speed. This book explains the physiological basis of plyometrics. It discusses where the system originated, why it is used, and how to make it work for you.

Much of the information on plyometrics to date has been anecdotal or methodologically weak. In the hands of the uninformed, any system of exercise can be misused. I intend here to dispel the myths and correct the misinformation about plyometrics. I will show you how plyometrics fits into a complete training program (for plyometrics was never intended to be "the only answer" in athletic training). Rather, plyometric training should be a progressive continuum. It starts simply, and as the athlete matures and develops physically, the system becomes more complex and skill-specific.

I believe that there are two kinds of physical work: hard work and smart work. I classify plyometric training as smart work. In the hands of the knowledgeable coach and athlete, plyometrics can produce movements that are quick, explosive, and fast-reacting. It can truly be a piece of the elite performance puzzle.

# CHAPTER 1

# UNDERSTANDING PLYOMETRICS

This chapter describes the development of plyometric training and the methods by which athletes have experienced significant improvement in performance through using plyometrics. I cover the physiology of plyometrics along with the relationship of other fitness variables, such as flexibility and aerobic and anaerobic training, to plyometric training programs.

## THE DEVELOPMENT OF PLYOMETRIC TRAINING

Plyometrics is the term now applied to exercises that have their roots in Europe, where they were first known simply as *jump training.*

Interest in this jump training increased during the early 1970s as East European athletes emerged as powers on the world sport scene. As the Eastern bloc countries began to produce superior athletes in such sports as track and field, gymnastics, and weight lifting, the mystique of their success began to center on their training methods.

The actual term *plyometrics* was first coined in 1975 by Fred Wilt, one of America's more forward-thinking track and field coaches. Based on Latin origins, *plyo + metrics* is interpreted to mean "measurable increases." These seemingly exotic exercises were thought to be responsible for the rapid competitiveness and growing superiority of Eastern Europeans in track and field events.

Plyometrics rapidly became known to coaches and athletes as exercises or drills aimed at linking strength with speed of movement to produce power. Plyometric training became essential to athletes who jumped, lifted, or threw.

During the late 1970s and into the '80s, those in other sports also began to see the applicability of these concepts to their own movement activities. Throughout the 1980s, coaches in sports such as volleyball, football, and weight lifting began to use plyometric exercises and drills to enhance their training programs. If there was any drawback to this enthusiasm, it lay with the lack of expertise that American coaches and athletes had in administering plyometric programs and a faulty belief that more must be better. Since these early growth years, however, practitioners have learned through applied research, as well as trial and error, to establish realistic expectations.

## HOW PLYOMETRICS WORKS

Plyometrics is defined as exercises that enable a muscle to reach maximum strength in as short a time as possible. This speed–strength ability is known as power. Although most coaches and athletes know that power is the name of the game, few have understood the mechanics necessary to develop it. To help you understand plyometrics, I'll review some of the important points of muscle physiology. This will serve to demonstrate the simple, yet complex, way in which plyometric training relates to better performance.

## Physiology of Muscles

Muscles, along with bones, provide for posture and movement in the human body. Muscles are our only musculoskeletal structures that can lengthen and shorten. Unlike the other supporting structures, ligaments and tendons, muscles possess a unique ability to impart dynamic activity to the body. (Ligaments are tough, dense, fibrous tissues that attach bone to bone to provide both support and mobility. Tendons are the very fibrous structures that attach muscles to bones.)

Two types of muscle fiber make up muscles: extrafusal and intrafusal. Extrafusal fibers contain myofibrils, the elements that contract, relax, and elongate muscles. Myofibrils are made up of several bands, and between the bands are units called sarcomeres. Sarcomeres contain myofilaments made up of the proteins actin and myosin. The myosin myofilaments have small projections, called cross-bridges, extending from them (see Figure 1.1). Extrafusal fibers receive nerve impulses from the brain that cause a chemical reaction. This reaction eventually causes the cross-bridges in the myosin to collapse and allows the actin and myosin myofilaments to slide over one another and the muscle fiber to shorten, or contract.

Intrafusal fibers, also called muscle spindles, lie parallel to the extrafusal fibers. Muscle spindles are the main stretch receptors in muscle. When a muscle

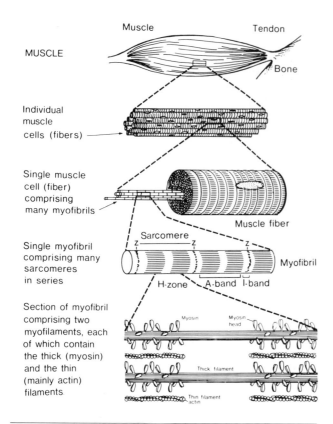

MUSCLE

Muscle                    Tendon

Bone

Individual
muscle
cells (fibers)

Single muscle
cell (fiber)
comprising
many myofibrils

Muscle fiber

Single myofibril
comprising many
sarcomeres
in series

Sarcomere
Z          Z          Z
Myofibril
H-zone    A-band   I-band

Section of myofibril
comprising two
myofilaments, each
of which contain
the thick (myosin)
and the thin
(mainly actin)
filaments

Myosin    Myosin
           head

Thick filament

Thin filament
actin

**Figure 1.1** The architecture of the muscle. *Note*. From *Lore of Running* (3rd ed.) by T. Noakes, 1991, Champaign, IL: Leisure Press. Reprinted by permission.

is stretched, the muscle spindles receive a message from the brain that initiates a stretch reflex.

Muscles derive their information from the central nervous system, or brain. This information travels through the spinal cord out into the peripheral nervous system, which extends out from the spinal cord, between the vertebrae, and ultimately to every muscle in the body. Among the messages reaching the muscles are those governing the length of each muscle at any point, the expected tension necessary for maintaining posture and initiating or stopping movement. An unbelievable amount of information is processed in each second.

## Types of Muscle Contractions

In sport activity the athlete has to be concerned with three modes of muscle contraction: eccentric, isometric, and concentric.

Eccentric contractions, which occur when the muscle lengthens under tension, are used to decelerate the body. In a runner's stride, for example, the impact of contacting the ground on a single foot requires the body's center of gravity to drop rapidly. The runner does not collapse at this moment because the leg muscles can contract and control this lowering motion.

Midstance in the stride, the body comes to a complete halt and an isometric contraction occurs, a static position in which there is no muscle shortening visible to the observer. In sport activities, this contraction occurs in the brief instant between the eccentric contraction and the subsequent concentric contraction, in which the muscle fibers pull together and shorten. This concentric contraction then results in acceleration of the limb segments in running.

## Using Knowledge of Muscle Physiology in Training

Eccentric (lengthening) muscle contractions are rapidly followed by concentric (shortening) contractions in many sport skills. Whenever a long jumper makes contact with the takeoff board, for example, there is an absorption of the shock of landing marked by slight flexion of the hip, knee, and ankle, followed by a rapid extension of the takeoff foot and leg as the jumper leaves the board.

Or think about the basketball player who drives for the slam dunk. As the player takes the last step toward the basket, the supporting leg must take the full body weight and stop the horizontal inertia of the run-up. This "loads" the leg by rapidly forcing its muscles to stretch and undergo a rapid eccentric contraction. Nerves firing information to the muscle then cause a concentric contraction. These muscle responses occur with no conscious thought on the part of the player; but without them, the player's knee would buckle and the player would collapse to the floor.

Another way of thinking about these muscle actions is to imagine a spring. In the case of the basketball player, the run-up puts pressure on the takeoff leg, compressing the coils of the spring. The energy stored within the spring is then released as the athlete leaves the floor.

Research from studies examining great jumpers and sprinters or other athletes who rely on the speed and strength capability of muscles shows that these athletes do not spend much time on the ground. These elite athletes have learned that energy is stored during the eccentric phase of muscle contraction and is partially recovered during the concentric contraction. However, the potential energy developed in this process can be lost (in the form of heat generation) if the eccentric contraction is not immediately followed by a concentric contraction. This conversion from negative (eccentric) to positive (concentric) work was described in the European literature as the *amortization phase*. This coupling of the eccentric–concentric contraction takes place within hundredths of a second. Typically, great high jumpers are on the ground a mere 0.12 seconds!

An entire system of exercise—plyometrics—has arisen just to address the development of a shorter amortization phase. And, perhaps surprisingly, the length of the amortization phase is largely dependent on learning. Where strength and innate speed are important, an athlete can shorten the amortization phase by applying learning and skill training to a base of strength development.

## Physiology of Plyometrics

Because the term plyometrics is a later creation, much of the early related physiological research is described by other names. The term used by researchers in Italy, Sweden, and the Soviet Union for this type of muscle action was the *stretch–shortening cycle*.

The physiological research supporting plyometrics, or the stretch-shortening cycle of muscle tissue, has been reviewed by many authors. The consensus of opinion cites the importance of two factors: (a) the serial elastic components of muscle, which include the tendons and the cross-bridging characteristics of the actin and myosin that make up the muscle fibers; and (b) the sensors in the muscle spindles (proprioceptors) that play the role of presetting muscle tension and relaying sensory input related to rapid muscle stretching for activation of the "stretch reflex."

Muscle elasticity is an important factor in understanding how the stretch-shortening cycle can produce more power than a simple concentric muscle contraction. As illustrated in the earlier descriptions of jumping, the muscles can briefly store the tension developed by rapid stretching so that they possess a sort of potential elastic energy. For an analogy, consider a rubber band—whenever you stretch it, there exists the potential for a rapid return to its original length.

The stretch reflex is another mechanism integral to the stretch-shortening cycle. A common example of the stretch reflex is the knee jerk experienced when the quadriceps tendon is tapped with a rubber mallet. The tapping causes the quadriceps tendon to stretch. That stretching is sensed by the quadriceps muscle, which contracts in response.

The stretch, or myotatic, reflex responds to the rate at which a muscle is stretched and is among the fastest in the human body. The reason for this is the direct connection from sensory receptors in the muscle to cells in the spinal cord and back to the muscle fibers responsible for contraction. Other reflexes are slower than the stretch reflex because they must be transmitted through several different channels (interneurons) and to the central nervous system (brain) before a reaction is elicited.

The importance of this minimal delay in the stretch reflex is that muscle undergoes a contraction faster during a stretch-shortening cycle than in any other method of contraction. A voluntary or thought-out response to muscle stretch would be too late to be of use to an athlete jumping, running, or throwing.

Besides response time, response strength is a consideration when determining how plyometrics relates to sport performance. Although the response time of the stretch reflex remains about the same even after training, training changes the strength of the response in terms of muscle contraction. The faster a muscle is stretched or lengthened, the greater its concentric force after the stretch. The result is a more forceful movement for overcoming the inertia of an object, whether it is the individual's own body weight (as in running or jumping) or an external object (a shot put, a blocking bag, an opponent, etc.).

## FLEXIBILITY

Anyone undertaking a plyometric training program should have a reasonable amount of flexibility. *Static stretching*, which increases flexibility, uses passive techniques to change the structures of ligaments, tendons, and muscles. The muscle is put into a stretched position and held for 6 to 15 seconds (sometimes more); this is then repeated three times.

*Ballistic stretching* involves elongating a muscle to its normal length and then bouncing gently against the end of the range 6 to 12 times, then repeating this action three times. Although research has shown static stretching techniques to be as effective as and possibly safer than ballistic stretching, ballistic stretching is still a valuable means of increasing range of motion.

Each method has its benefits, and in light of the principles of eliciting the stretch reflex and the serial elastic components of muscle to perform jumping activities, it might behoove the athlete to "prime" the mechanism by doing controlled ballistic stretching.

## AEROBIC TRAINING

Aerobic capacity is a valuable component of most fitness programs. However, plyometric training, by the nature of the energy systems being utilized, is not intended to develop aerobic capacity. Plyometric training is strictly anaerobic (without oxygen) in nature and utilizes the creatine phosphate energy system, allowing maximum energy to be stored in the muscle before a single explosive act, using maximum power, is performed. It is a program that exploits a quality of movement compatible with single repetition, maximal efforts. Recovery should be complete between each repetition of the exercise and between each set of repetitions. If sufficient recovery is not allowed, then the activity may move toward being aerobic, but quality of movement and explosiveness are sure to suffer.

## SUMMARY

1. There are three types of muscular contractions:
   - Eccentric
   - Isometric
   - Concentric
2. For an exercise to be truly plyometric, it must be a movement preceded by an eccentric contraction. This results not only in stimulating the proprioceptors sensitive to rapid stretch, but also in loading the serial elastic components (the tendons and cross-bridges between muscle fibers) with a tension force from which they can rebound.
3. A reasonable amount of flexibility is important when beginning a plyometric training program. Two types of stretching can be used to develop flexibility:
   - Static
   - Ballistic
4. Plyometric training is not intended to develop aerobic capacity and therefore requires complete recovery between reps and sets.

# CHAPTER 2

# THE BASICS OF PLYOMETRIC TRAINING

Now that you understand the inner workings of the muscular system and how they can be manipulated to create faster movements, let's turn our attention to exercises and drills that will create this change.

This chapter categorizes various plyometric exercises and explains the effects that can be achieved by using them. Plyometric training can take many forms, including jump training for the lower extremities and medicine ball exercises for the upper extremities. The user of plyometrics should understand not only how to do the exercises, but also how to implement and modify a program and use it to its best advantage.

## JUMP TRAINING EXERCISES

Early jump training exercises were classified according to the relative demands they placed on the athlete. But all of them can be progressive in nature, with a range of low to high intensity in each type of exercise. The classifications I use in this book are similar to those used by the Europeans. You should note, however, that early writings from the Soviet Union classified ''hops'' and ''jumps'' on the basis of distance rather than type of exercise. Hops were exercises performed for distances less than 30 meters, while jumps were performed for distances greater than 30 meters. This classification can become confusing, so in this book the words *hop* and *jump* are used interchangeably.

## Jumps-in-Place

A jump-in-place is exactly that: a jump completed by landing in the same spot where the jump started. These exercises are relatively low intensity, yet they provide the stimulus for developing a shorter amortization phase by requiring the athlete to rebound quickly from each jump. Jumps-in-place are done one after another, with a short amortization phase.

## Standing Jumps

A standing jump stresses single maximal effort, either horizontal or vertical. The exercise may be repeated several times, but full recovery should be allowed between each effort.

## Multiple Hops and Jumps

Multiple hops and jumps combine the skills developed by jumps-in-place and standing jumps; they require maximal effort but are done one after another. These exercises can be done alone or with a barrier. An advanced form of multiple hops and jumps is the box drill (described later). Multiple hops and jumps should be done for distances of less than 30 meters.

## Bounding

Bounding exercises exaggerate normal running stride to stress a specific aspect of the stride cycle. They are used to improve stride length and frequency. They typically are performed for distances greater than 30 meters.

## Box Drills

Box drills combine multiple hops and jumps with depth jumps (see the next section). They can be low in intensity or extremely stressful, depending on the height of the boxes used. They incorporate both horizontal and vertical components for successful completion.

## Depth Jumps

Depth jumps use the athlete's body weight and gravity to exert force against the ground. Depth jumps are performed by stepping out from a box and dropping to the ground, then attempting to jump back up to the height of the box. Because depth jumps are of a prescribed intensity, one should never jump (rather than step) from the top of the box, as this adds height and increases the landing stress. Controlling the height dropped helps not only to accurately measure intensity but also to reduce overuse problems. Upon making contact with the ground, the athlete directs the body up as fast as possible. The key to performing this exercise and decreasing the amortization phase is to stress the ''touch and go'' action off the ground.

### Research on Depth Jumps

There seems to have been a fascination with studying the depth jump. The early Soviet research concluded that depth jumps were an effective means of increasing athletes' speed and strength capabilities. Verhoshanski (1969) proclaimed 0.8 meters as the ideal height for achieving maximum speed in switching from the eccentric to the concentric phase of the stretch-shortening cycle and 1.1 meters for developing maximal dynamic strength. He also recommended no more than 40 jumps in a single workout, performed no more than twice a week. Recovery between sets was facilitated by light jogging and calisthenics.

A later study by Verhoshanski and Tatyan (1983) comparing three groups of athletes showed that depth jumps were more effective than weight training, the jump-and-reach, or horizontal hops for developing speed and strength capabilities. Other researchers, such as Adams (1984), Bosco and Komi (1979), and Asmussen et al. (1974), have sought the optimal height for depth jumps. Over a dozen studies conducted in the United States and Europe have served only to confuse the issue.

### Proper Depth-Jump Height

In practical terms, the task of determining a proper depth-jump height centers on the ability to achieve maximal elevation of the body's center of gravity after performing a depth jump. If the height is too great for the strength of the legs, then the legs spend too much time absorbing the impact of the landing and cannot reverse the eccentric loading quickly enough to take advantage of the serial elastic component of muscle and the stretch reflex phenomenon. The result is a slow jump dependent on strength and devoid of power. Coach and athlete should work to find the proper height, one that lets the athlete maximize the height jumped plus achieve the shortest amortization phase.

One method described by many authors for determining maximum depth-jump height is outlined in the box.

### Benefits of Depth Jumps

Research conducted in the United States since the late 1970s has shown that depth jumps generally increase athletes' abilities to jump higher in test situations. Any conflicts in the research about the effects of depth jumps are probably due to the many experimental designs that have been used.

The simplicity of performing the depth jump has made it an easy task to study. Investigators have tried to relate depth jumps to improvements in start speed, acceleration, and absolute speed in running and jumping but have tended to ignore the more elusive role of horizontal jump training (standing jumps, multiple jumps, and bounding). But because running and jumping involve both horizontal and vertical components, it seems to make sense that both horizontal and vertical jump training would contribute to improvements in both activities.

## WHERE TO TRAIN

Plyometric training is quite versatile. It can be performed indoors or out—the basic requirements are ad-

---

### How to Determine Maximum Depth-Jump Height

1. The athlete is measured as accurately as possible for a standing jump-and-reach. (See page 31 for instructions on how to do a standing jump-and-reach.)

2. The athlete performs a depth jump from an 18-inch box height, trying to attain the same standing jump-and-reach score.

3. If the athlete successfully executes this task, he or she may move to a higher box. The box height should be increased in 6 inch increments. Step 2 is repeated until the athlete fails to reach the standing jump-and-reach height. This then becomes the athlete's maximum height for depth jumps.

4. If the athlete cannot reach the standing jump-and-reach height from an 18-inch box, either the height of the box should be lowered or depth jumping abandoned for a time in favor of strength development. If the athlete cannot rebound from a basic height of 18 inches, he or she probably does not have the musculoskeletal readiness for depth jumping.

equate space and a "yielding" landing surface (with some give to prevent jarring the lower extremities with excessive force). Resilite wrestling mats, spring-loaded gymnastics or aerobics floors, and grass or synthetic playing fields are all possibilities for landing pads.

As far as space is concerned, it need simply be free of obstructions. Gym floors, large weight rooms, and outdoor fields are all suitable environments so long as the landing surface is appropriate.

## EQUIPMENT

A significant advantage to plyometric training is that it requires so little prefabricated equipment. The following represents the ultimate list of needed items.

### Cones

Plastic cones (Figure 2.1) ranging in height from 8 to 24 inches serve as barriers over which to jump. The flexibility of cones makes them less likely to cause injuries if landed directly upon.

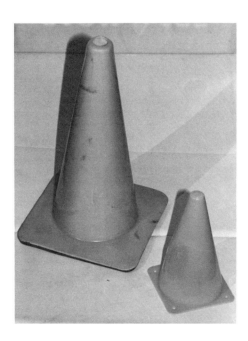

**Figure 2.1**  Plastic cones.

### Boxes

Boxes do need to be specially constructed, but they are far from complex in their design. A variety of boxes, constructed of 3/4-inch plywood or a similar flexible yet durable wood, are needed. Boxes should range in height from 6 to 24 inches (with greater

heights up to 42 inches only for elite athletes with strong weight-training backgrounds). The boxes also need adequate landing (top) surfaces of at least 18 by 24 inches. Figure 2.2 shows a standard plyometric box.

**Figure 2.2**  A standard plyometric box.

Landing surfaces must also be made nonslip, by attaching treads like those used on stairways, by mixing sand into the paint used to cover the boxes, or by gluing carpeting or rubberized flooring to the landing surfaces.

Numerous variations of the plyometric box have been developed over the years:

- *Adjustable boxes* (Figure 2.3)—boxes that can be altered to accommodate the varying abilities of athletes.

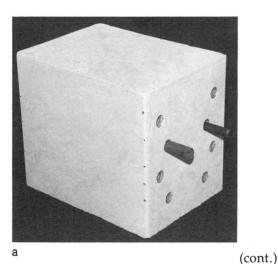

a                                                    (cont.)

**Figure 2.3**  An adjustable plyometric box: (a) The base, and (b) fully assembled.

b

**Figure 2.3**   Continued.

- *Storage boxes* (Figure 2.4)—boxes that can double as storage containers. (If one side is left open, the box needs to be constructed very sturdily on the remaining sides.)

**Figure 2.4**   A storage box.

- *Special effects boxes* (Figure 2.5)—built to provide a special type of exercise stimulus. The most common of these is an *angle box*, which emphasizes the small muscles of the ankle and lower leg. The angle box is used to prevent ankle injuries by teaching athletes to learn to land on irregular surfaces. It is also useful in the rehabilitation of ankle and knee injuries.

**Figure 2.5**   A special effects box (angled).

In schools, physical education and athletic departments can often collaborate with industrial arts departments to build plyometric boxes. This is cost effective and can promote a camaraderie between departments as students see their products being put to use.

## Hurdles and Barriers

Most school physical education programs own hurdles and barriers. Hurdles, which are adjustable for degree of difficulty, do represent a hazard because of their rigid construction, and they should be used only by experienced plyometric exercisers (see Figure 2.6).

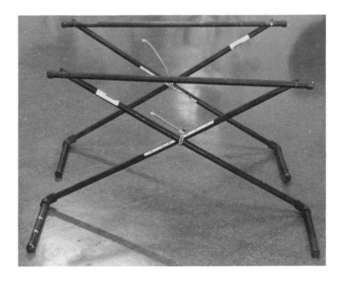

**Figure 2.6**   Standard hurdles.

Foam barriers (Figure 2.7) are manufactured for gymnastics and tumbling. Barriers can also be constructed by scoring Styrofoam sheets on one side and then folding them to form soft triangular obstacles.

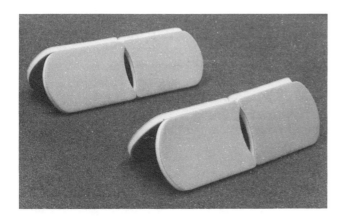

**Figure 2.7**  Foam barriers.

Barriers can also be formed simply by balancing a wooden dowel (1/2-inch diameter and 3 feet long) on top of two cones (Figure 2.8).

**Figure 2.8**  A cone-and-dowel barrier.

## Stairs

Stairways, bleachers, and stadium steps are all usable for plyometric training, with one word of caution: Inspect them carefully to make sure they are safe for jumping. Concrete steps are undesirable for jumping because they are unyielding surfaces.

## Medicine Balls

These weighted objects (Figure 2.9) are useful for upper body exercises and in combination with lower extremity training. They should be easily gripped, durable, and of varying weights to accommodate those of all strength levels.

**Figure 2.9**  Medicine balls.

## TRAINING CONSIDERATIONS

Plyometric training can be structured to individuals or to groups. Individual training requires exercisers to perform every task to the best of their ability (according to their level of development). It focuses on responsibility, concentration, and follow-through to complete the training session.

Group achievement can be structured so as to encompass, in addition to physical skills, social skills like communication, cooperation, trust, and immediate and long-term feedback in goal setting and achievement. Both individual and group sessions should take place in an environment that is positive in nature and emphasizes individual development.

There are several considerations in implementing a plyometric training program, whether for an individual or a group. The most important of these are common sense and experience. Programs must be prudently planned and administered. One of the major tasks is to conduct a needs analysis, taking into account the athlete's sport and the specific movements the athlete must perform to participate effectively. The needs analysis is covered in more depth in chapter 3. Other issues to consider are the athlete's age, experience, and athletic maturity.

The responsibility in initiating a plyometric program is enormous. The best coaches do not always win with their athletes, but they do make training an enjoyable, organized, and progressive activity that ultimately leads the athlete to higher levels of performance.

## Sex

The myth that females must train differently than males still exists in some circles. But there is no reason that female athletes cannot perform plyometrics with the same degree of skill, proficiency, and intensity as males. The controlling factor of having a strength base is applicable to both sexes. Any athlete who chooses to ignore complementary strength training is headed for difficult times and perhaps injury. It is true that many female athletes are new to strength training and thus may not possess the requisite entry-level abilities. It is the responsibility of the coach and the athlete to upgrade this area of development before attempting plyometric training.

## Age

The simple factor of attention span is probably the major consideration in starting youngsters in plyometric training programs. Children will always run and jump as a part of play. But as adults we tend to take this element of play (known also as "fun"!) out of training programs by rigidly applying specific regimens.

### The Young Athlete

Elementary school children can successfully do plyometric training as long as the coach does not call it *plyometrics*. Children of this age need images, such as animals in the forest jumping over streams and logs, to relate to. They can visualize and cognitively grasp the ease and skill with which a deer bounds through the woods. If movement patterns are placed in the proper context, children can attempt to express them in a "plyometric" fashion. In fact, hop-scotch is a great early plyometric drill!

### The Pubescent Athlete

Young athletes can benefit more from direct training as they approach pubescence. They can begin to relate more to sport situations and see the correlation between what the coach asks them to do and their development in their sport.

Plyometrics for this group should always begin as gross motor activities of low intensity. They should be introduced into warm-ups and then added to sport-specific drills.

### The Mature Athlete

As athletes approach the stage of individualization, they can begin to look at developing off-season and preseason training programs as preparation for performance. For most athletes this will be upon reaching high school, although in certain activities (ice skating, gymnastics, swimming, diving, dance, and track and field) the coach and the athlete may need to begin developing training cycles that use regimented plyometrics at an earlier age. This also depends on the athlete's level of competition.

## Training Level

Two considerations regarding training level are important when structuring a plyometric training program: the intensity level of the exercise and the experience of the athlete. Plyometric training should be a progression of exercises and skilled movements that are considered to be elementary, intermediate, and advanced in scope. They should focus on improving the ballistic and reactive skills of the exerciser and are to be considered stressful. Drills should be evaluated for intensity before they are incorporated into a workout. Examples of low-, moderate-, and high-intensity drills may be found in chapter 4. Categorizing exercises by intensity helps both in choosing starting points for exercise and in developing program progression.

Another factor in program design is the training level of the athlete. Though this may sound obvious, consider that one of the early European writings on jump training stated that the athlete had to perform squats with 2.5 times their body weight before starting plyometrics—if every 150-pound athlete had to demonstrate squat strength of 375 pounds, there would be very few athletes doing plyometrics!

Practical experience has shown that many athletes benefit from plyometrics without demonstrating such leg strength. The exercise must be geared to the individual. An athlete who is barely past pubescence and is relatively unskilled should be considered a beginner. Beginners should be placed in a complementary resistance training program and should progress slowly and deliberately into a program of low-intensity plyometrics such as skipping drills, 8-inch cone hops, and box drills from 6 to 12 inches.

High school competitors who have been exposed to weight-training programs can benefit from moderately intense plyometrics. And accomplished, mature, college-level athletes with strong weight-training backgrounds should be able to perform ballistic-reactive exercises of high intensity with no undue problems. Once a classification of beginner, intermediate, or advanced has been generally determined, one can begin to plan a program.

## Eccentric Strength

Eccentric strength, or the ability of a muscle to lengthen while under tension, is an important consideration for all athletes and is crucial for injured ones. Given that healthy limbs often have difficulty sustaining the impact placed on the body during practice and competition, it is essential that injured athletes returning to activity have some means of ensuring a safe and complete return.

Physical therapists and other rehabilitation specialists are beginning to recognize the importance of eccentric strength in rehabilitating musculoskeletal injuries. Research has shown that eccentric strength is crucial to the return of injured athletes to their sports.

Eccentric strength is a precursor to success in plyometrics. Before an injured athlete can return to plyometric training there has to be an interval of training that focuses on the development of stability and eccentric strength in the lower extremities. Resistance training that isolates a single joint (open kinetic chain activities) and relegates it to performing single plane movements will not "rehabilitate" the athlete sufficiently to return her or him to activity. Simply put, you do not play the game sitting in a chair. Closed kinetic chain activities, which require the athlete to use the lower extremities in functional movement patterns involving the foot, ankle, knee, and hip have risen to the top of the list of effective rehabilitation exercises. Plyometric training also falls into the realm of closed kinetic chain activities.

Plyometric drills and skill activities can serve as functional tests to determine an injured athlete's readiness for return to play. The environment of competition places tremendous mental and physical stress on participants, and not being sure of one's physical ability is to risk a disastrous performance and, worse, reinjury. One recent study (Drez, 1987) cited single leg hops for a distance and timed single leg hops of 6 meters (about 20 feet) as a major determinant in the recovery of injuries to the anterior cruciate ligament in the knee. The ability to complete this task revealed a great deal about whether an athlete was truly ready to return to play. A below-normal score on these single leg hop tests indicated a knee at risk of giving way during sport activities. A passing score is determined by a symmetry score of 85%. The involved leg is tested twice and the average between the two trials is recorded. Then the noninvolved leg is tested in the same way. The scores of the noninvolved extremity are divided by the scores of the involved leg and multiplied by 100. This constitutes the symmetry index score, recorded as a percentage.

## Specificity of Training

Plyometric training is very specific in nature but very broad in applicability. For the lower extremities, it is designed to train the athlete to develop either vertical or horizontal acceleration, and all movements in running and jumping are simply the exertion of some vertical or horizontal force against the ground. Even changes of direction fall into this category. Medicine ball exercises train the upper extremities and can also be used in combination with lower extremity training.

Specificity is a key concept, then, to keep in mind when planning a plyometric training program. The sport and the skill to be developed must be analyzed so proper exercises can be emphasized. To develop start speed from a crouch position, like an offensive lineman might assume, it doesn't make sense to spend a lot of time on depth-jump skills, which develop vertical power. A more worthwhile exercise might be the standing long jump or double leg hops, which develop horizontal force.

Or perhaps the goal is to improve a basketball player's rebounding ability. Analyzing rebounding reveals that the skills needed are to react quickly in a vertical motion and to repeat jump height (because the first jump may not succeed in getting the rebound). This player, then, need not invest lots of time in jumps that emphasize horizontal abilities, such as double leg hops or bounds. Chapter 3 explains how to develop a program with these considerations in mind.

## SUMMARY

1. There are six classifications of lower extremity plyometric exercises:
   - Jumps-in-place
   - Standing jumps
   - Multiple hops and jumps
   - Bounding
   - Box drills
   - Depth jumps

     Medicine ball exercises train the upper extremities.

2. The following basic equipment is needed to conduct a plyometric training program:
   - Cones
   - Boxes
   - Hurdles or barriers
   - Stairs
   - Medicine balls

3. The most important consideration in implementing and administering a plyometric training program is the athlete. Age, experience, and athletic maturity are all important criteria in establishing and modifying plyometric training.

4. Eccentric strength development is important for all athletes, and particularly so for injured athletes.

5. Plyometric training can be adapted to virtually every sport, and athletes should do exercises that help to enhance the movements they perform. By mimicking certain movements in plyometric training, athletes can decrease movement time and become more powerful.

# CHAPTER 3

# DESIGNING A PLYOMETRIC TRAINING PROGRAM

Now that you have a grasp of the basics, let's turn our attention to actually designing a plyometric training program. An art form as well as a science, this manipulation of variables can either create a champion or foster an also-ran.

This chapter will cover the factors of plyometric training program design. It will discuss some of the concepts relevant to developing a basic, a sport-specific, or an advanced program.

The information on developing a sport-specific program includes two sample 4-week training programs, along with the rationale for creating them, one addressing vertical jumping ability and the other linear jumping ability. Granted, 4 weeks is only a fraction of a training year, but the sample programs should give you insight into the process of designing programs.

## VARIABLES OF EXERCISE

Any training program should begin with a period of preparation and move into time frames, or cycles, with specific goals. An example would be a 6-week cycle that begins with a pretest and has the goal of increased distance in the standing triple jump. The cycle would end with a posttest to see if the goal was achieved. An effective program accomplishes specific goals through the manipulation of four variables: intensity, volume, frequency, and recovery.

### Intensity

Intensity is the effort involved in performing a given task. In weight lifting, intensity is controlled by the amount of weight lifted. In plyometrics, intensity is controlled by the type of exercise performed. Plyometrics ranges from simple tasks to highly complex and stressful exercises. Starting out with skipping is much less stressful than alternate bounding. Double leg hops are less intense than single leg bounds.

The intensity of plyometric exercises can be increased by adding light weights in certain cases, by raising the platform height for depth jumps, or simply by aiming at covering a greater distance in longitudinal jumps. Other writers have rated the intensity of various plyometric exercises from low to very intense

(see Stone & O'Bryant, 1987). The exercises in this book are rated low to high. Any attempt to classify exercises by intensity is imperfect at best, but the guidelines provided here should help you in your program design. Figure 3.1 depicts the scale of intensity for jump training exercises.

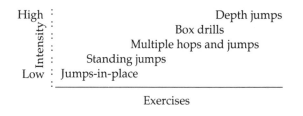

**Figure 3.1** Intensity scale for jump training exercises.

## Volume

Volume is the total work performed in a single workout session or cycle. In the case of plyometric training, volume is often measured by counting foot contacts. For example, an activity like the standing triple jump, comprised of three parts, counts as three foot contacts. Foot contacts provide a means of prescribing and monitoring exercise volume.

The recommended volume of specific jumps in any one session will vary with intensity and progression goals. Table 3.1 shows sample exercise volumes for beginning, intermediate, and advanced workouts. A beginner in a single workout in an off-season cycle could do 60 to 100 foot contacts of low-intensity exercises. The intermediate exerciser might be able to do 100 to 150 foot contacts of low-intensity exercises and another 100 of moderate-intensity exercises in the same cycle. Advanced exercisers might be capable of 150 to 250 foot contacts of low- to moderate-intensity exercises in this cycle.

The volume of bounding (exaggerated running) activities is best measured by distance. In the early phases of conditioning, a reasonable distance is 30 meters per repetition. As the season progresses and the abilities of athletes improve, the distance may be progressively increased to 100 meters per repetition.

**Table 3.1   Number of Foot Contacts by Season for Jump Training**

| | Beginning | Inter-mediate | Advanced | Intensity |
|---|---|---|---|---|
| | | Level | | |
| Off-season | 60-100 | 100-150 | 120-200 | Low-Mod |
| Preseason | 100-250 | 150-300 | 150-450 | Mod-High |
| In-season | — | Depends on sport | — | Moderate |
| Championship Season | — | Recovery only | — | Mod-High |

Low-intensity exercises used during warm-ups are generally not included in the number of foot contacts when computing volume. Thus warm-ups should stay low in intensity and progressive in nature so they do not overextend the athlete.

## Frequency

Frequency is the number of times an exercise is performed (repetitions) as well as the number of times exercise sessions take place during a training cycle.

Research on frequency in plyometrics is obscure. There seems to be no conclusive evidence that one frequency pattern is *the* means of increasing performance. Practical experience and some European writings have led me to believe that 48 to 72 hours of rest is necessary for full recovery before the next exercise stimulus, although the intensity of the exercises has to be considered. Skipping as a plyometric exercise is not as stressful as bounding and will not require the same amount of recovery time. Beginners should have at least 48 hours of recovery between plyometric sessions. If the athlete does not get enough recovery, muscle fatigue results in the athlete's being unable to respond to the exercise stimuli (ground contact, distance, height) with maximal, quality efforts. The overall result is less efficient training for athletic development.

There are varied methods for establishing frequency in plyometric training. Some coaches prefer to use a Monday and Thursday schedule during the preparation cycle (see Table 3.2). Using the principle of 48 to 72 hours of recovery for lower extremity training, one can easily see the many program variations that can be developed. Running programs can also be integrated into the training cycle along with or replacing weight training on certain days, although it is recommended that weight training be a priority in developing and maintaining the strength base neces-

sary to carry out a successful plyometric training program.

Because of the stressful nature of plyometrics and the emphasis on quality of work, plyometric exercises should be performed before any other exercise programs. They can be integrated into weight training (this combination, called *complex training*, is described later in this chapter) at a later cycle in the training year if desired, or they might comprise the entire workout. This is quite conceivable, in fact, if the athlete is involved in track and field, where the plyometric training might be very specific to the event or to skill development.

**Table 3.2   Samples of Frequency of Off-season or Preseason Plyometric Training**

| | Program 1 | Program 2 | Program 3 |
|---|---|---|---|
| Monday | Weight training | Plyometrics (lower extremities) | Plyometrics (lower extremities) |
| Tuesday | Plyometrics (lower extremities) | Weight training | Plyometrics (upper extremities—medicine ball) |
| Wednesday | Weight training | Plyometrics (upper extremities—medicine ball) | Running program |
| Thursday | Plyometrics (lower extremities) | Weight training | Plyometrics (lower extremities) |
| Friday | Weight training | Plyometrics (lower extremities) | Rest |

## Recovery

Recovery is a key variable in determining whether plyometrics is developing power or muscular endurance. For power training, longer recovery periods (45 to 60 seconds) between sets, or groupings of multiple events, such as a set of 10 rim jumps, allow maximum recovery between efforts. A work:rest ratio of 1:5-1:10 is required to assure proper execution and intensity of the exercise. Thus, if a single set of exercises takes 10 seconds to complete, 50-100 seconds of recovery should be allowed. Remember, plyometric training is an anaerobic activity. Shorter recovery periods (10 to 15 seconds) between sets do not allow for maximum recovery and develop muscular endurance.

Less than 2 seconds of recovery time in exercise of 12 to 20 minutes makes a workout aerobic. Exercise for both strength and endurance is usually achieved through circuit training, where the athlete continues from one exercise to another without stopping between sets.

The preparation (off-season) cycle for a plyometric program should involve general gross motor exercises, such as skipping for coordination or simple jumping, without specific skill training, like change of direction. As the preseason cycle approaches, exercises should become more specific to the sport.

If the sport itself is specific to plyometric training, as in long, high, and triple jumping, plyometrics can be carried through the in-season cycle. However, for sports dominated by vertical jumping, like basketball and volleyball, it may be advisable to reduce the amount of plyometric training to a level consistent with the development of the athlete. For example, a professional basketball team that plays a schedule of three or more games a week with constant travel may find it impossible to train plyometrically during the season. On the other hand, the Men's National volleyball team conducts plyometric training of up to 400 jumps while training during the season because they play a limited match schedule. Common sense must play a role in determining whether the athlete should continue plyometrics in season.

## USING PLYOMETRICS WITH OTHER TRAINING

Jump training and upper body plyometrics are relevant to many sports. Gymnastics, jumping events in track and field, diving, and volleyball are all arenas where success depends on the athlete's ability to explode from the standing surface and generate vertical velocity, linear velocity, or both to achieve the desired result.

But plyometrics is not a panacea in athletic conditioning. It does not exist in a vacuum, nor should it be thought of as a singular form of training. Instead, plyometrics is the icing on the cake, to be used by athletes who have prepared their tendons and muscles through resistance training for the tremendous impact forces imposed in high-intensity plyometrics.

Anaerobic conditioning, in the form of sprint or interval training, is essential to developing the stride patterns required in proper plyometric bounding. The explosive reactions of sprinting or of movement drills that require changes of direction can be performed as interval training (repeated efforts with measured recovery periods).

Done together, resistance training and anaerobic training help prepare the athlete's body for plyometrics. In turn plyometrics enhances the athlete's ability to perform in resistance exercise and anaerobic activity: a true partnership in athletic training.

## Resistance Training

Resistance training is the ideal counterpart of plyometric training, for it helps prepare the muscles for the rapid impact loading of plyometric exercises. In resistance training one works to develop the eccentric phase of muscle contraction by first lowering the body or weight and then overcoming the weight using a concentric contraction.

"Open-chain" resistance training (using machines that isolate a single joint) is useful for developing strength in specific muscle groups. However, the user of plyometrics also needs to perform "closed chain" exercises that involve multijoint activities such as free weight exercises (using barbells, dumbbells, and a medicine ball). These exercises, which are generally performed with the feet fixed to the ground as in squatting, are more functional for athletes, allowing them to assume positions specific to their sports when they exercise. Closed chain exercises have proven themselves to have much higher carryover value than isolated joint exercises in developing athletic ability.

Plyometric training can be successfully integrated with resistance training by imposing a speed–strength task immediately on muscles that have been subjected to pure strength movements like those in weight lifting (see the discussion of complex training on page 23).

The more intense plyometric exercises become, the more crucial the need for strength. As mentioned earlier, some of the early European literature spoke of the need to squat 2.5 times body weight before undergoing a training program. There is no doubt that those authors had a high-intensity program in mind, but a strength requirement is part and parcel of plyometric training at all levels.

Parameters that are used to determine if an athlete is strong enough to begin a plyometric program may center more on functional strength (including power) testing than the traditional one-repetition maximum (1RM) squat that measures pure strength. One such test has been used by a number of practitioners in plyometric training programs. As a test of power more than strength, it may have more direct applicability.

Weight equal to 60% of the athlete's body weight is placed on a squat bar, and the athlete is asked to perform five repetitions in 5 seconds, tested against a stopwatch. If the athlete cannot do so, emphasis should be given to a resistance training program and the intensity of the plyometric training program should remain low to moderate.

Poor strength in the lower extremities results in loss of stability when landing, and high-impact forces are excessively absorbed by the soft tissues of the body. Early fatigue also becomes a problem without adequate leg strength. Together, these will result in the deterioration of performance during exercise and an increased chance for injury (as in any overuse situation).

## Anaerobic, Sprint, and Interval Training

Plyometrics trains two anaerobic energy systems, the creatine phosphate and the lactic acid cycles. The creatine phosphate system depends on energy stores that already exist in the muscles. Plyometric exercises that last a mere 4 to 15 seconds deplete the energy stores. When designing a program to train the creatine phosphate system, a considerable amount of rest or recovery should be allotted between exercises; the emphasis is on quality of work, not quantity. The lactic acid threshold is reached when the muscles' energy stores have been exhausted by the creatine phosphate system. Exercise that proceeds past the point of using the energy stores taxes the lactic acid threshold. Exercise bouts at near-maximal effort that last around 30 to 90 seconds are appropriate for training that system.

In general, jumps-in-place, standing jumps, and depth jumps are short-duration activities used to train the creatine phosphate system. Multiple jumps, box drills, and particularly bounding can qualify as exercises for training the lactic acid threshold.

It is beneficial to train the creatine phosphate system in athletes involved in sports that require quick bursts of power with long recovery periods between performances, such as long jump or triple jump. Training the lactic acid threshold is helpful for athletes in sports like football or volleyball where activity is fairly prolonged and rest periods are more infrequent.

Sprint and interval training are running programs that require the athlete to perform quality efforts in training for a certain amount of time (usually around 30 to 90 seconds) with prescribed recovery periods. This type of training is closely related to plyometric training of the lactic acid threshold but uses sprints instead of multiple jumps, box drills, or bounding exercises.

## Circuit Training

One of the many benefits of plyometric training is that it can be organized into circuits. By moving from sta-

tion to station (see Figure 3.2 for a sample circuit), the athlete can do a variety of exercises that stress either the vertical or linear components of various movement patterns, or both.

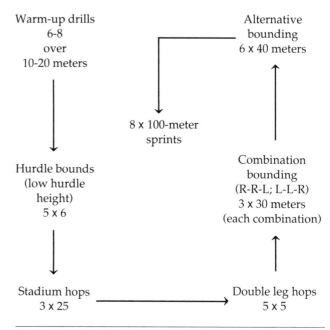

**Figure 3.2**  Sample circuit.

By using circuits, athletes can perform activities of even greater duration than with anaerobic, sprint, and interval training. This may move the level of cardiovascular stress toward improvement in aerobic conditioning, resulting in increased stamina. The cumulative effect of circuit training is considerable, so the recovery period should be at least 2 days.

## DESIGNING A BASIC PROGRAM

A basic plyometric program might be intended for the novice or the young athlete. It should follow the rules of safety and the considerations set forth in chapter 2. If the program is intended for the more advanced athlete, the same rules apply, but the exercises become more complex and more intense. The following considerations affect the design of training programs at any level.

## Testing and Assessment

I cannot, of course, attempt to detail the hundreds of physical tests that exist in sport. But it is important to know that testing (data collection) and assessment (comparing the gathered data to establish performance standards) of an athlete before and after training periods, or cycles, is vital to both measuring improvement and providing direction and motivation. Goal setting should be a way of life for athletes and coaches. Most athletes respond positively to definable goals and reasonable standards.

Standard tests of physical fitness, such as the 300-yard shuttle, the standing vertical jump, and the standing long jump, are good for gathering baseline data. These or similar test scores should be recorded for future reference. More advanced athletes can be tested on skills such as the standing triple jump or the single leg hop over 25 meters.

Plyometric training should be a means of improving self-image and self-realization. Athletes should be concerned with competing against themselves and should be encouraged to do as well as they can in training as well as testing. Testing should be done both before and after training modules to let athletes rate themselves against their own accomplishments as well as against established norms.

For athletes in individual events, such as track and field or swimming, the ultimate posttest is the competition itself—even more so during the championship season. It is there that the time spent in preparation, planning, and performance can culminate in that moment of synthesis known as *peaking*.

## Movement Skills

Beginners should be taught the concepts behind plyometric activities, including the importance of eccentric versus concentric strength. The importance of the stretch-shortening cycle (the countermovement of the legs) in the ability to start quickly should be stressed.

Feet should be nearly flat in all landings. The ball of the foot may touch first, but the rest of the foot should also make contact. Landing should be reversed quickly; the object is to spend minimal time on the ground.

For the arms to help develop force into the ground to ''compress the spring,'' elbows must be brought behind the midline of the body so the arms can be brought rapidly forward and up as the concentric contraction occurs for liftoff. This movement is the double arm swing.

Initial activities should be of lower intensity (see chapter 4 for examples) and preparatory. The coach must be aware of the progression needed in both intensity and skill requirement.

## Time Allocation

Actual exercise time in a beginning plyometric program should not exceed 20 to 30 minutes. An additional 10 to 15 minutes each should be devoted to a warm-up and a cool-down that emphasize stretching

and low-intensity movement activities. Warm-ups can start with passive stretching and walking and progress to skipping, light jogging, and side-to-side movements, using big arm swings to warm up the shoulders. Cool-downs should focus on low-stress activities such as light jogging, stretching, and walking. Advanced athletes may do longer workouts to perform longer drills, requiring greater recovery.

## Plyometric Activity

The actual number of jumps to be implemented in any program depends on many variables. Remember that this is a sample program, and your particular situation might call for variation. Refer to the information on intensity, frequency, volume, and recovery earlier in this chapter. The key guiding concepts are *prudence* and *simplicity*.

Some variables concern whether an athlete is involved in complementary resistance or weight training. An athlete without prior experience generally should not perform plyometric and resistance training on the same day. An experienced athlete who wishes to combine plyometrics and resistance training should do plyometrics first to allow for maximal response from muscles not fatigued by prior exertions. Plyometrics and weight training can also be effectively combined by advanced or elite athletes in complex training (page 23).

Another concern regarding plyometric training is the timing of the athletic season. In the off-season or preseason, training should progress toward more intense exercises. To supplement in-season training, conditioning levels should be maintained using exercises of low to moderate intensity.

Prudence in prescribing and performing plyometric exercise has to do with when and how much training is done. A hard, skill-oriented sport practice should not be followed by a high-volume, high-intensity plyometric workout. More will be accomplished by using warm-up and low-intensity plyometric work to allow for recovery. Even better would be devoting a single training day to plyometrics to provide variety and allow physiological and mental recovery from skill practice.

## Length of Cycle

The length of time spent in any single training cycle depends on the days per week available before the start of the season. With beginning athletes, the emphasis should be on skill development, not on progression to higher intensity exercises. Twelve to 18 weeks of a basic plyometric program is advised to ensure that athletes can properly execute the mechanics of plyometric activities before they attempt higher volumes and intensities of exercise. This is compatible with the off-season and preseason cycles of training format discussed under the topic of volume in this chapter.

## Safety

Probably the most important safety consideration to remember is that more is not necessarily better. If a workout has been accomplished with apparent ease, go back to the drawing board for future workouts. Don't impulsively add more exercises that day just because there's no visible fatigue. Remember that quality, not quantity, is the goal in plyometric training.

The abilities and body composition of the individual also affect the safety of training. Large, heavy athletes should not perform single leg activities until they have fully adjusted to the stress of plyometric training. It would not be unusual for such athletes to do double leg jumps for an entire season before developing the necessary strength for more complex activities (standing triple jumps, single leg hops, etc.). This same conservative philosophy applies to young athletes without strength or jump training experience.

Staying physically healthy is a must we take for granted, but it requires planning. Coaches must make sure that their plyometric training programs do not increase an athlete's chances of injury. Often injuries occur when muscles are tired—at the end of practice or when the coach asks for ''just one more.'' Fatigue takes away from the sharpness of senses, and the athlete is probably just going through the motion of the exercise. Sprained ankles and twisted knees are among the common trauma associated with a lack of control due to excessive fatigue. This is the time when prudence is particularly important.

A final safety consideration concerns the *overload principle*. In extending this principle to plyometrics, coaches ask, ''Should athletes use weights when they jump?'' It is *not* advisable for beginning athletes to use any weighted vests, belts, or bands. Although the earlier European writings describe the use of added weight (up to 10% of body weight), this was with elite athletes with years of experience in training and competition. And even these athletes were not continuously subjected to this regimen. Adding weight should be done with caution, only after a long preparation period, and no more than once a week for an 8-week cycle.

## THE SPORT-SPECIFIC PROGRAM

Creating a sport-specific program requires understanding the mechanics of the sport by doing a needs analysis, breaking down skill patterns into their most elementary parts. For example, a volleyball spike depends largely on being able to make a short approach, convert horizontal movement into vertical lift, and perform a swinging motion at the top of the jump. Plyometric work, then, should focus on developing the vertical component of jumping. But a football running back, by contrast, must develop great horizontal acceleration from a static start and needs tremendous lateral hip strength for rapid changes of direction. In plyometric training, 80% of total foot contacts should apply to activities that closely resemble the skills necessary for success in the sport; the remaining 20% can apply to general conditioning.

As an athlete develops, so will the ability to use plyometrics. A long or triple jumper, for example, often uses plyometric training for both conditioning and skill development because the event is close to the exercise itself. It is not unusual for a college triple or long jumper to start out bounding 300 total meters per exercise session and by midseason do 1,500 total meters of bounding in a single workout.

In other sports, such as basketball, volleyball, tennis, and football, various jump drills can be integrated with skill patterns to approximate what happens on the court or field. Table 3.3 shows what skills are developed by which jump.

## SAMPLE PROGRAMS FOR INCREASING VERTICAL AND LINEAR JUMPS

To show you more specifically how to design a program to meet your needs, I've written two specific sample programs, one that develops vertical jumping and another that develops linear jumping. The sample programs are based on the specific needs of the hypothetical athletes described, so they are not to be applied universally. But you can adapt the principles to design programs specific to your needs.

## Vertical Jump

There is a five-step procedure that can be followed to improve vertical jump. For the sake of brevity, this sample program covers only 4 weeks of a training cycle.

### Step 1: Consider the Athlete

James is a 16-year-old basketball player with 1 year of varsity experience. He has had 2 years of resistance training in the high school football coach's weightlifting class. He has sprained an ankle in the past, but he is healthy at this time.

**Table 3.3  Skills Built by Plyometric Exercises**

| Skill | Jumps-in-place | Standing Jumps | Multiple Jumps | Box Drills | Bounding | Depth Jumps |
|---|---|---|---|---|---|---|
| Start speed | √ | √ | √ | | | √ |
| Acceleration | | | √ | √ | √ | |
| Change-of-direction | | √ | √ | √ | | √ |
| Vertical jump | √ | √ | √ | √ | | √ |
| Horizontal jump | | √ | √ | √ | √ | |

## Step 2: Assess and Test the Athlete

For developing vertical jump, measure the following abilities.

1. *Standing jump-and-reach.* Standing on both feet, James reaches as high as he can on a wall; mark that height. Then James jumps off both feet and reaches as high on the wall as he can; again mark the height. Record the difference between the two marks.
2. *Jump from box.* James does a depth jump from an 18-inch box. After he lands, he jumps up and reaches as high on a wall as he can; record the height of the touch.
3. *Three-step vertical jump.* James takes three steps and on the final step (which should be with his preferred foot) jumps up and reaches as high on a wall as he can; mark the height of the jump.
4. *One-repetition maximum parallel squat.* James determines the maximum amount of weight he can lift one time doing a back squat. To do the squat, James stands with his back to a barbell that is resting on a rack at should height, lifts the barbell to rest on his shoulders, bends at the hips and knees until his thighs are parallel to the floor, and returns to the starting position.
5. *Five-repetition/5-second parallel squat at 60% body weight.* James performs five squats with a barbell, weighted equal to 60% of his body weight. He attempts to do the squats within 5 seconds.

The test results dictate the type and direction of the program. For James, Tests 4 and 5 indicate adequate

strength because his 1RM squat was 1.5 times his body weight, and he could squat 5 times in 5 seconds with 60% of his body weight. If these scores had been below standard (he could squat only 75% of his body weight and took 7.5 seconds to complete five squats at 60% of his body weight), it would indicate that resistance work is still a major requirement of training or even a prerequisite to undergoing high-intensity plyometrics. Strength work alone might increase vertical jump if James were deficient.

Tests 1, 2, and 3 show James's present vertical jumping ability and give data against which to measure his progress at the end of the program. James reached 21 inches in the standing jump-and-reach, 18 inches in the jump from box, and 20 inches in the three-step jump-and-reach (indicating that he isn't any better off one foot than two).

## Step 3: Consider the Time Frame or Cycle

James's program will be for 4 weeks. The program has been condensed from a normal periodized training year to demonstrate the preparation, progression, and performance variables involved in program design. At the end of this cycle, James is retested to check for progress.

## Step 4: Select the Time in the Training Year

James will follow his program during the month of September, before the onset of the season and at the time when most high school athletes in winter sports begin to make an effort to get in shape.

## Step 5: Design the Program

Plan each of the 4 weeks according to three variables:

1. Preparation
2. Progression
3. Performance

### Week 1

*Preparation:* Use high-volume, low-intensity resistance training and low-intensity plyometrics to allow the body's soft tissues to accommodate to the stress of jumping and the impact of landing.

*Progression:* Include enough variety to challenge the athlete to learn new skills.

*Performance:* Concentrate on proper landing techniques and the use of the arms in performing low-intensity exercises. Make sure the concept of the amortization phase is understood.

*Workout Schedule:* (Remember, this is a hypothetical program. The following schedule pertains only to James.)

Monday, Wednesday, Friday: Weight training

3 × 12 (3 sets of 12 repetitions) parallel squats with 70% 1RM (1 repetition maximum, or 70% of the maximum weight James is able to lift one time)

split squats with 50% of body weight

inverted leg presses

push presses (front)

shrug pulls

Tuesday: Plyometrics

1 × 10 two-foot ankle hops

side-to-side ankle hops

hip-twist ankle hops

split squat jump

standing jump-and-reaches

Thursday: Plyometrics

1 × 10 two-foot ankle hops

side-to-side ankle hops

hip-twist ankle hops

2 × 10 rim jumps

2 × 20 single leg push-offs from a 12-inch box

2 × 20 alternating push-offs from a 12-inch box

## Week 2

*Preparation:*  Use resistance training to stress basic strength in the lower extremities.

*Progression:*  Integrate higher levels of intensity into plyometric exercises to add complexity and intensity to resistance training.

*Performance:*  Remember that quality, not quantity, is the key in performing plyometric exercises.

*Workout Schedule:*

Monday: Plyometrics

3 × 10 front box jumps (18-inch box)

1 × 10 standing jump over barrier (36 inches)

3 × 3 double leg hops

2 × 10 rim jumps

3 × 10 two-foot ankle hops

Tuesday: Weight training

3 × 8 front squats

4 × 8 inverted leg presses

2 × 8 push presses (front)

2 × 8 high pulls

Wednesday: Weight training

5 × 5 back squats with 70% to 80% 1RM

Thursday: Plyometrics

3 × 10 side-to-side ankle hops

3 × 10 single leg push-offs

3 × 10 front box jumps (18-inch box)

3 × 10 rim jumps

1 × 5 standing triple jumps

Friday: Weight training

Repeat Tuesday's workout, but replace the push presses with behind-the-neck push presses.

## Week 3

*Preparation:*  Emphasize heavy plyometric work. Use resistance training as a form of recovery.

*Progression:*  Concentrate on building basic strength in those muscle groups associated with plyometric exercises for vertical jumping. Continue to build on both volume and intensity.

*Performance:*  Emphasize quality of effort by applying time and distance goals (e.g., How quickly can the athlete accomplish 1 × 10 side-to-side box shuffles? How far can the athlete travel when performing standing triple jumps?).

*Workout Schedule:*

Monday: Plyometrics

3 × 10 depth jumps (from 18-inch box)

3 × 10 standing jumps over barrier (18 to 24 inches)

3 × 5 double leg hops

3 × 10 single leg hops with cone

3 × 10 side-to-side ankle hops

Tuesday: Weight training

4 × 5 front squats

4 × 8 inverted leg presses

3 × 8 behind-the-neck push presses

3 × 5 stiff knee cleans

Wednesday: Weight training

3 × 8 hamstring curls—Concentric: Raise weight with both legs

Eccentric: Lower weight with one leg

5 × 5 back squats with 85% to 90% 1RM

Thursday: Plyometrics

3 × 10 box jumps (18-inch box)

1 × 3 standing triple jumps

3 × 10 lateral jumps over barrier (12 to 18 inches)

3 × 10 alternating push-offs

3 × 10 rim jumps

Friday: Weight training

Repeat Tuesday's workout, but substitute split squats for front squats.

## Week 4

*Preparation:* Emphasize low-volume, high-intensity exercises. Neuromuscular preparation is directed toward maximal efforts with full recovery in both plyometrics and weight training.

*Progression:* The challenge is to work toward maximal efforts in plyometrics. Maximal vertical efforts with minimal ground contact time are a must.

*Performance:* Resistance training as well as plyometrics should now be focused on power. The concept of maximal force applied rapidly is the key to developing vertical jump.

*Workout Schedule:*

Monday: Plyometrics

    3 × 10 depth jumps (from 18-inch box)

    3 × 10 standing jumps over barrier (18 to 24 inches)

    3 × 10 single leg hops over cone

    3 × 10 double leg hops

Tuesday: Weight training

    5 × 3 quarter-squats

    5 × 5 inverted leg presses

    3 × 8 ham curls

    5 × 3 front squats to push presses

Wednesday: Plyometrics

    3 × 10 depth jumps to 24-inch or higher box

    3 × 10 alternating push-offs

    3 × 10 lateral jumps over cone (12 to 18 inches)

    3 × 10 rim jumps

Thursday: Weight training

Repeat Tuesday's workout, but add 5 × 3 power cleans from the thigh hang position.

Friday: Retest

In our theoretical model of training the results of the re-testing might look like this: James is tested again on the tasks that he did at the beginning of the cycle, to check for improvement. After implementing the 4-week training James scores 22 inches for the standing jump-and-reach, 22.5 inches for the depth jump-and-reach, and 23 inches for the three-step jump-and-reach. As the training year continues, James should try to maintain his improved vertical jumping ability, and perhaps even increase it more. Future workouts will be designed according to his new goals.

## Linear Jump

The same five-step procedure for improving vertical jump applies to linear jumping.

### Step 1: Consider the Athlete

Connie is an 18-year-old college freshman with a mark of 36'0" in the triple jump. She has had high school experience as a triple and long jumper but has been average at best. She has no injuries or physical limitations.

### Step 2: Assess and Test the Athlete

For improving linear jump, measure present ability with the following linear events.

1. *Standing triple jump for distance.* Connie stands on her preferred foot; she hops, steps, and jumps into a pit. Measure the distance from the start of the jump to the landing.

2. *Five double leg hops for distance.* Taking off from and landing on both feet at the same time, Connie hops five times to see how much distance she can cover. Measure the distance from the start to the landing on the fifth hop.

3. *Flying 30 meters for time.* To measure the flying 30, the coach needs to mark off 100 meters on the track. The athlete gradually builds up speed over the first 60 meters. The athlete is then timed between the 60 to 90 meter marks; this measures the athlete's absolute speed.

4. *One-repetition maximum parallel squat.* Connie determines the maximum amount of weight she can lift one time doing a squat in the same way that James did (p. 19).

5. *Five-repetition/5-second parallel squat at 60% body weight.* Again imitating the technique described for James, Connie attempts to perform five squats in 5 seconds.

Connie's test results will indicate her ability and readiness to undertake a high-intensity plyometric training program. Connie's scores on Tests 4 and 5 show she meets the basic strength criteria. If she were deficient, it would be important to emphasize weight training for 4 to 6 weeks before undertaking intensive plyometric training.

Tests 1, 2, and 3 show Connie's present linear jumping ability and give data against which to measure her progress at the end of the program. Connie jumped 7 meters (23 feet) on the standing triple jump, covered 7.9 meters (26 feet) on the double leg hops, and had a flying 30 meters time of 3.4 seconds.

## Step 3: Consider the Time Frame or Cycle

Connie's program takes place over a 4-week period. The program has been condensed from a normal periodized training year to demonstrate the preparation, progression, and performance variables involved in program design.

## Step 4: Select the Time in the Training Year

Normally a track athlete would begin training at the start of school in the fall. However, Connie will be involved in a crash course of training during the 4 weeks in February. She needs to prepare for the first outdoor meet that takes place at the beginning of March.

## Step 5: Design the Program

Plan each of the 4 weeks according to three variables:

1. Preparation
2. Progression
3. Performance

## Week 1

*Preparation:* Use high-volume, low-intensity resistance training and low-intensity plyometrics to allow the body's soft tissues to accommodate to the stress of linear jumping and the impact of landing.

*Progression:* Emphasize variety in the type of plyometrics used, and review the skills of linear jumping.

*Performance:* Concentrate on proper landing techniques and the use of the arms in performing low-intensity exercises. Make sure the concept of the amortization phase is understood.

*Workout Schedule:*

Monday: Weight training

    3 × 12 parallel squats with 70% 1RM

    push presses (front)

    lat pulls

    split squats with 50% body weight

    hamstring curls—Concentric: Raise weight with both legs
        Eccentric: Lower weight with one leg

Tuesday: Plyometrics

    1 × 10 front cone hops (18 inches)

    2 × 20 single leg push-offs (12-inch box)

    2 × 20 alternating push-offs (12-inch box)

    2 × 30 second segments of the 90 second box drill

    2 × 10 front box jumps (12-inch box)

    3 × 3 double leg hops

Wednesday: Weight training

    3 × 12 front squats

        inverted leg presses

        incline bench presses

        split squats with 50% body weight

        calf raises

Thursday: Plyometrics

    2 × 10 front cone hops (18 inches)

    3 × 3 double leg hops

    1 × 5 standing triple jumps

    3 × 40 yards submaximal alternate bounding with double arm action

Friday: Weight training

Repeat Monday's workout, but add 3 × 10 shrug pulls.

## Week 2

*Preparation:* Weight training should emphasize work for hip adductors and abductors, as well as the hip flexors and hip extensors.

*Progression:* Many dynamic jumps should be done while moving across the ground.

*Performance:* Linear jumping skill includes synchronizing arms with lower extremities to maximize efforts.

*Workout Schedule:*

Monday: Plyometrics and weight training

    3 × 10 front cone hops (18 inches)

    3 × 5 double leg hops

    1 × 5 standing triple jumps over barrier

    3 × 40 yards alternate bounding with double arm action

    3 × 8 split squats

    3 × 8 lat pulls

    3 × 8 hamstring curls

    3 × 8 inverted leg presses

    3 × 8 behind-the-neck presses

Tuesday: Rest

Wednesday: Weight training

    3 × 8 lunges

    3 × 8 high pulls

    3 × 8 front shoulder raises with dumbbells

    3 × 8 parallel squats with 80% to 85% 1RM

Thursday: Plyometrics

    3 × 15 stadium hops

    3 × 40 yards combination bounding with double

arm action

5 × 5 barrier hops (hurdle hops)

3 × 5 double leg hops (for distance)

Friday: Weight training

3 × 8 lunges

lat pulls

inverted leg presses

high pulls

front push presses

## Week 3

*Preparation:* Resistance training becomes more ballistic, with continued emphasis on performing lifts in positions similar to the joint angles reached in linear jumping.

*Progression:* Plyometric training becomes more complex, yet is task-specific. Running speed is a consideration in this phase of training.

*Performance:* Emphasis on plyometric training skills should be on distance, time, or both.

*Workout Schedule:*

Monday: Weight training

4 × 5 front squats to push presses

stiff knee cleans

inverted leg presses

4 × 10 split squat walk (exchange legs and move forward)

3 × 10 pulley weights, hip flexion (to work on knee drive)

Tuesday: Plyometrics

3 × 20 stadium hops

5 × 3 double leg hops into 40-yard sprints

3 × 5 standing long jumps (for distance)

3 × 10 single leg hops

3 × 40 yards alternate bounding

Wednesday: Weight training

5 × 5 back squats with 90% 1RM

Thursday: Rest

Friday: Plyometrics and weight training

5 × 6 multiple box-to-box squat jumps (18- to 24-inch boxes)

5 × 40 yards combination bounding

5 × 60 yards alternate bounding with double arm action

3 × 8 depth jumps to standing long jumps

Repeat Monday's weight-training workout.

## Week 4

*Preparation:* Resistance training and plyometrics should now focus on power. Low-volume and high-intensity are the keys in both forms of training.

*Progression:* Single leg activities are of the highest intensity in plyometric training. Along with depth jumps, these become a vital part of development.

*Performance:* Quality of effort will yield maximal distances in the shortest times during this cycle.

*Workout Schedule:*

Monday: Plyometrics and weight training

5 × 20 stadium hops

5 × 5 barrier hops (hurdle hops)

3 × 50 yards combination bounding

3 × 40 yards single leg bounding

1 × 6 long jumps with a five-stride approach

5 × 3 parallel squats with 90% to 95% 1RM

3 × 8 hamstring curls

5 × 3 inverted leg presses

3 × 8 overhead squats (snatch grip)

Tuesday: Rest

Wednesday: Weight training

5 × 3 power cleans from the thigh hang position

Thursday: Plyometrics

1 × 10 depth jumps to standing triple jumps with slide out landing

1 × 10 depth jumps to standing long jumps

5 × 40 yards alternate bounding with double arm action (timed with stopwatch)

5 × 30 yards combination bounding into sand pit

Friday: Retest

Connie is tested again on the tasks that she did at the beginning of the program, to check for improvement. After implementing this 4-week program Connie scores 7.9 meters (26 feet) on the standing triple jump, covers 8.1 meters (30 feet) on the double leg bounds, and flying 30 meters time is 3.2 seconds. As the track season continues, Connie should try to continue to improve her linear jumping ability.

## COMPLEX TRAINING

You may have wondered by now whether weight training and plyometrics can ever be done in the same workout. Yes, they can—by athletes who are experienced in weight training and have also been through basic jump training. Early European writings labeled this combination *complex training*. Complex training occurs when you alternate weight training and plyometrics within the same workout session.

Combining strength movement exercises like squats with speed movements like the standing triple jump can be a very effective way to stimulate the neuromuscular system and provide variety for the athlete. Combining the bench press with the "power drop" (a medicine ball exercise) is an example of upper extremity complex training.

In complex training, the volume of plyometric exercises should be reduced to a number that is easily workable between sets of the particular lift. For instance, an athlete might alternate sets of six half-squats with five standing triple jumps, then five double leg hops, then five depth jumps from an 18-inch box. This method of training should be used with the major weight lifts—squats, inverted leg presses, split squats, bench presses, power cleans, snatches, and push presses. As a rule of thumb, integrating two major lifts with plyometrics during a workout should yield maximum results. Trying to do any more than this usually requires too much time and brings the possibility of fatigue and overtraining.

## SUMMARY

1. There are four exercise variables to manipulate in accomplishing specific training goals:
   - Intensity
   - Volume
   - Frequency
   - Recovery
2. Plyometrics is a training method to be used with the other methods:
   - Resistance training
   - Anaerobic, sprint, and interval training
   - Circuit training
3. A number of issues should be considered when developing a basic plyometric training program:
   - The athlete's training level (determined through testing and assessment)
   - The athlete's movement skills
   - Time available
   - The amount of plyometric activity to be included
   - Training cycle length
   - Safety
4. Vertical and linear jumping ability can be improved by carefully constructed, sport-specific plyometric training programs.
5. Complex training combines strength movement exercises and plyometric exercises to improve sport skills.

# CHAPTER 4
# PLYOMETRIC EXERCISES

This chapter explains 90 different techniques that fall into the seven different plyometric exercise categories listed in chapter 2. For each exercise, you will be told what equipment you need, the starting position, and the action sequence required. The exercises within each category are arranged according to intensity level—from low to high.

## KEY TO SYMBOLS

The symbols next to the exercise name show you what sports or activities can benefit most from that exercise and the exercise's intensity level. Following is a key to the symbols.

## Sports or Activities

 Baseball and Softball

 Basketball

 Bicycling

 Diving

 Downhill Skiing

 Figure Skating

 Football

 Gymnastics

 Ice Hockey

 Soccer

 Swimming

 Tennis

 Track and Field: Jumping Events

 Track and Field: Sprints

 Track and Field: Throwing Events

 Volleyball

 Warm-Up

 Weight Lifting

 Wrestling

## Intensity Rating

Low
Low to Moderate
Moderate
Moderate to High
High

# JUMPS-IN-PLACE

Two-Foot Ankle Hop

Single Foot Side-to-Side Ankle Hop

Side-to-Side Ankle Hop

Hip-Twist Ankle Hop

Tuck Jump With Knees Up

Tuck Jump With Heel Kick

Split Squat Jump

Split Squat With Cycle

Split Pike Jump

Straight Pike Jump

## Two-Foot Ankle Hop

### Equipment:
None.

### Start:
Stand with feet shoulder-width apart and the body in a vertical position.

### Action:
Using only the ankles for momentum, hop continuously in one place. Extend the ankles to their maximum range on each vertical hop.

## Single-Foot Side-To-Side Ankle Hop

### Equipment:
Two cones placed 3 to 4 feet apart.

### Start:
Stand on one foot between the cones.

### Action:
Hopping from one foot to the other, land on the right foot next to the right cone, then the left foot next to the left cone. Continue hopping back and forth.

## Side-to-Side Ankle Hop

### Equipment:
None.

### Start:
Stand with feet shoulder-width apart and the body in a vertical position.

### Action:
Covering a span of 2 to 3 feet, jump side to side, producing the motion from the ankles. Keep the feet shoulder-width apart and land on both feet at the same time.

## Hip-Twist Ankle Hop

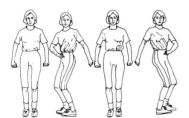

### Equipment:
None.

### Start:
Stand with feet shoulder-width apart and the upper body in a vertical position.

### Action:
Hop up and twist from the hips, turning the legs in a 180-degree arc. On the next hop, turn the legs to return to the starting position. Continue turning the legs from side to side on each hop. The upper body does not turn; the movement comes from the hips and legs.

## Tuck Jump With Knees Up

### Equipment:
None.

### Start:
Stand with feet shoulder-width apart and the body in a vertical position; do not bend at the hips.

### Action:
Jump up, bringing the knees up to the chest and grasping the knees with the hands before the feet return to the floor. Land in a standing vertical position, without any forward bend. Repeat the jump immediately.

## Tuck Jump With Heel Kick

### Equipment:
None.

### Start:
Stand with feet shoulder-width apart and the body in a straight vertical position with arms by your sides.

### Action:
Keeping the knees pointed down (still in line with the body), jump and kick the buttocks with the heels. Repeat the jump immediately. This is a quick-stepping action from the knees and lower legs. Swing the arms up as you jump.

## Split Squat Jump

### Equipment:
None.

### Start:
Spread the feet far apart, front to back, and bend the front leg 90 degrees at the hip and 90 degrees at the knee.

### Action:
Jump up; using arms to help lift, hold the split-squat position. Land in the same position and immediately repeat the jump.

## Split Squat With Cycle

### Equipment:
None.

### Start:
Standing upright, spread the feet far apart, front to back, and bend the front leg 90 degrees at the hip and 90 degrees at the knee.

### Action:
Jumping up, switch leg positions—the front leg kicks to the back position and the back leg bends up and comes through to the front. While bringing the back leg through, try to flex the knee so that it comes close to the buttock. Land in the split-squat position and jump again immediately.

## Split Pike Jump

### Equipment:
None.

### Start:
Start with feet shoulder-width apart and the body straight.

### Action:
Jump up and lift the legs up and out to each side. Attempt to touch your toes at the height of the jump, then return to starting position. You should attempt to keep you legs straight. Try to keep jumps going in repeat fashion.

## Straight Pike Jump

### Equipment:
None.

### Start:
Stand with the feet shoulder-width apart and the body straight.

### Action:
Jump up and bring the legs up together in front of the body; flexion should occur only at the hips. Attempt to touch your toes at the peak of the jump. Return to starting position and repeat.

# STANDING JUMPS

Standing Long Jump

Standing Jump-and-Reach

Standing Jump Over Barrier

Lateral Jump With Two Feet

1-2-3 Drill

Straddle Jump to Camel Landing

Standing Long Jump With Lateral Sprint

Lateral Jump With Single Leg

Lateral Jump Over Barrier

Standing Long Jump With Sprint

Standing Long Jump With Change of Direction

Standing Triple Jump

Standing Triple Jump With Barrier Jump

## Standing Long Jump

### Equipment:

A soft landing surface, such as a mat or sand pit.

### Start:

Stand in a semisquat with feet shoulder-width apart.

### Action:

Using a big arm swing and a countermovement (flexing) of the legs, jump forward as far as possible.

## Standing Jump-and-Reach

### Equipment:

An object suspended overhead, or a wall with a target marked.

### Start:

Stand with feet shoulder-width apart.

### Action:

Squat slightly, and explode upward, reaching for a target or object. Do not step before jumping.

## Standing Jump Over Barrier

### Equipment:

One cone or hurdle.

### Start:

Stand with feet shoulder-width apart.

### Action:

Bending only at the hips, bring the knees up to jump over the barrier. Don't let the knees turn sideways or split apart to clear the object; the body should remain a straight line.

## Lateral Jump With Two Feet

### Equipment:

None.

### Start:

Stand with feet shoulder-width apart.

### Action:

Swing the leg on the side to which you are going to jump across the stationary leg. Swing the same leg out to the other side and jump in that direction as far as possible, landing on both feet. Then jump back to the starting position by reversing the process.

## 1-2-3 Drill

### Equipment:

A mark 40 meters from the start.

### Start:

Stand with one foot slightly in front of the other.

### Action:

Use three steps (left-right-left or right-left-right) in a continuous motion to simulate a takeoff; complete the three steps with a quick-quicker-quickest rhythm, then explode vertically off the last one. Emphasize the action of takeoff and make the motion crisp. As soon as you land after the jump, step right into the next sequence of steps; continue for 40 meters.

## Straddle Jump to Camel Landing

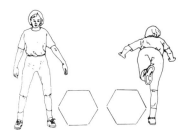

### Equipment:

A mat or flexible barrier.

### Start:

Stand with one foot in front of the other at an angle to the mat or barrier.

### Action:

Using an action similar to a straddle high jump, plant the takeoff foot at an angle to the barrier and use a straight lead leg swing to lift the body over the mat. This turns the front of your body so it straddles the mat. Land on the foot that cleared the mat first, and let the trailing leg swing over and in a straight line behind you. Hold your arms out to the side for balance as if you were a figure skater on skates.

## Standing Long Jump With Lateral Sprint

### Equipment:

Two marks, 10 meters to either side of a landing pit.

### Start:

Stand in a semisquat with feet shoulder-width apart.

### Action:

Using a big arm swing, do a standing long jump; land on both feet (try to stay upright). Immediately sprint laterally (right or left) for 3 meters.

## Lateral Jump With Single Leg

### Equipment:

None.

### Start:

Stand with feet shoulder-width apart.

### Action:

Jump up but push sideways to the left off the ground and land on your left foot. Immediately push off sideways to the right, landing on the left foot again. Continue pushing off from and landing on your left foot for the prescribed repetitions. Repeat this exercise using your other leg.

## Lateral Jump Over Barrier

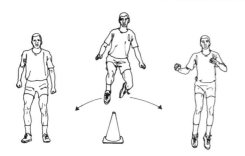

### Equipment:
One cone or hurdle.

### Start:
Stand alongside the object to be cleared.

### Action:
Jumping vertically but pushing sideways off the ground, bring the knees up to jump sideways over the barrier.

## Standing Long Jump With Sprint

### Equipment:
A mark 10 meters from the end of jump, and a mat, grass surface, or sand pit for landing.

### Start:
Stand in a semisquat with feet shoulder-width apart.

### Action:
Using a big arm swing, jump forward as far as possible. Upon landing sprint forward approximately 10 meters. Try to keep from collapsing on the landing; land fully on both feet, then explode into a sprint.

## Standing Long Jump With Change of Direction

### Equipment:
A mat or sand pit for landing and several marks 10 meters to either side of it.

### Start:
Stand in a semisquat with feet shoulder-width apart.

### Action:
Using a big arm swing, jump forward as far as possible. Upon landing, immediately sprint to one of the 10-meter marks.

## Standing Triple Jump

### Equipment:

A mat or sand pit.

### Start:

Stand with feet shoulder-width apart, 3 to 6 meters from a sand pit (distance depends on ability).

### Action:

Push off both feet simultaneously and extend through the hips to land on one foot (hop), then push from this foot forward to land on the other foot (step), then jump from that foot extending the feet forward as far as possible and landing with both feet in the pit or on a mat.

## Standing Triple Jump With Barrier Jump

### Equipment:

A barrier (a line of cones or a mat) just in front of a sand pit.

### Start:

Stand with feet shoulder-width apart, 3 to 6 meters from a sand pit (distance depends on ability).

### Action:

Push off both feet simultaneously and extend through the hips to land on one foot (hop), then push from this foot forward to land on the other foot (step), then jump from that foot over the barrier, extending the feet forward as far as possible.

# MULTIPLE JUMPS

Hexagon Drill

Front Cone Hops

Diagonal Cone Hops

Rim Jumps

Cone Hops With Change-of-Direction Sprint

Cone Hops With 180-Degree Turn

Double Leg Hops

Lateral Cone Hops

Barrier Hops (Hurdle Hops)

Stadium Hops

Single Leg Hops

Zig-Zag Drill

## Hexagon Drill

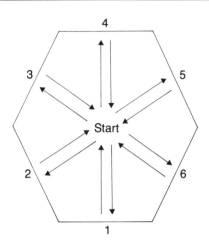

### Equipment:
A hexagon of tape on the floor, with sides about 24 inches long.

### Start:
Stand in the center of the hexagon with feet shoulder-width apart.

### Action:
Jump across one side of the hexagon and back to center, then proceed around each side of the hexagon. This may be done for a specific number of complete trips around the hexagon or for total time.

## Front Cone Hops

### Equipment:
A row of 6 to 10 cones or small barriers (8 to 12 inches tall) set up approximately 3 to 6 feet apart.

### Start:
Stand with feet shoulder-width apart at the end of the line of barriers (with their length spread out before you).

### Action:
Keeping feet shoulder-width apart, jump over each barrier, landing on both feet at the same time. Use a double arm swing and work to decrease the time spent on the ground between each barrier.

## Diagonal Cone Hops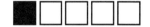

### Equipment:
A row of 6 to 10 cones or small barriers (8 to 12 inches tall) approximately 3 to 4 feet apart.

### Start:
Stand with feet together at the end of the line of barriers.

### Action:
Keeping ankles together, jump in a zig-zag fashion across the barriers, moving down the line. Land on the balls of the feet at the same time, and use a double arm swing to stabilize the body movement.

## Rim Jumps

### Equipment:

A high object such as a basket-ball goal or crossbar on a football goalpost.

### Start:

Stand with feet shoulder-width apart under the high object.

### Action:

Jump continuously, reaching with alternating hands and try-ing to reach the object on every jump. Time on the ground should be minimal, with each jump being, at least as high as the one before.

## Cone Hops With Change-of-Direction Sprint

### Equipment:

A partner and a row of four to six cones placed 3 to 4 feet apart to form a *Y*.

### Start:

Stand with feet shoulder-width apart facing the first cone. Part-ner stands at the top of the Y, between the two spread cones.

### Action:

Do two-footed hops over the row of cones; as you are clearing the last cone, your partner points to one of the far cones; sprint to that cone immediately upon landing from the last hop.

## Cone Hops With 180-Degree Turn

### Equipment:

A line of four to six cones spaced 2 to 3 feet apart.

### Start:

Stand facing forward, parallel to the line of cones, your feet even with the first.

### Action:

Jump. While in the air, turn 180 degrees, so that you land facing the opposite direction. Con-tinue to jump and turn in the air down the entire line of cones.

## Double Leg Hops

### Equipment:
None.

### Start:
Stand with feet shoulder-width apart.

### Action:
Squat down and jump as far forward as possible. Immediately upon touching down, jump forward again. Use quick double arm swings and keep landings short. Do in multiples of three to five jumps.

## Lateral Cone Hops

### Equipment:
Three to five cones lined up 2 to 3 feet apart (distance depends on ability).

### Start:
Stand with feet shoulder-width apart at the end of the line of cones (with cones stretched out to one side).

### Action:
Jump sideways down the row of cones, landing on both feet. In clearing the last cone, land on the outside foot and push off to change direction, then jump two-footed back down the row of cones sideways. At the last cone, push off again on the outside foot and change directions. Keep movement smooth and even, trying not to pause when changing directions.

# Barrier Hops (Hurdle Hops)

### Equipment:
Hurdles or barriers (between 12 to 36 inches) set up in a row, spaced according to ability. Barriers should be able to collapse if the athlete makes a mistake.

### Start:
Stand at the end of the line of barriers.

### Action:
Jump forward over the barriers with feet together. Movement comes from the hips and knees; keep the body vertical and straight, and do not let knees move apart or to either side. Use a double arm swing to maintain balance and to gain height.

# Stadium Hops

### Equipment:
Bleachers or stadium steps.

### Start:
Stand in a quarter-squat at the bottom of the stairs, with hands on hips or back of neck and feet shoulder-width apart.

### Action:
Jump to the first step and continue up for 10 or more jumps. Make landings light and quick; movements should be continuous up the stairs without pauses. Generally, the athlete should be able to take two steps at a time.

## Single Leg Hops

### Equipment:
None.

### Start:
Stand on one leg.

### Action:
Push off with the leg you are standing on and jump forward, landing on the same leg. Use a strong leg swing to increase length of jump, and strive for height off each jump. Immediately take off again after landing, and continue for 10 to 25 meters. Perform this drill on both legs for symmetrical development. Beginning athletes will use a straighter jump leg; advanced athletes should try to pull the heel towards the buttocks during the jump.

## Zig-Zag Drill

### Equipment:
Two parallel lines, 24 to 42 inches apart and 10 meters long.

### Start:
Stand balanced on one foot on a line.

### Action:
Jump from one line to the other in a continuous forward motion for 10 meters, always taking off and landing on the same foot. Do not "double hop" at the touchdown.

# BOX DRILLS

Alternating Push-Off

Single Leg Push-Off

Lateral Step-Up

Side-to-Side Box Shuffle

Front Box Jump

Lateral Box Jump

30-, 60-, or 90-Second Box Drill

Multiple Box-to-Box Jumps

Pyramiding Box Hops

Multiple Box-to-Box Squat Jumps

Multiple Box-to-Box Jumps With Single Leg Landing

## Alternating Push-Off

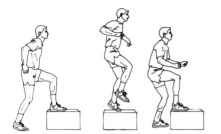

### Equipment:

A box 6 to 12 inches high.

### Start:

Stand on the ground and place one foot on the box, heel close to the closest edge.

### Action:

Push off of the foot on the box to gain as much height as possible by extending through the entire leg and foot; land with feet reversed (the box foot lands a split second before the ground foot). Use a double arm swing for height and balance.

## Single Leg Push-Off

### Equipment:

A box 6 to 12 inches high.

### Start:

Stand on the ground and place one foot on the box, heel close to the closest edge.

### Action:

Push off of the foot on top of the box to gain as much height as possible by extending through the entire leg and foot. Land with the same foot on top of the box and push off again. Use a double arm swing for height and balance.

## Lateral Step-Up

### Equipment:

A box 6 to 12 inches high.

### Start:

Standing to the side of the box, place the foot closest to the box on top.

### Action:

Use the leg on the box to raise the body until the leg is extended, then lower to starting position. Don't push off the foot on the ground; use the bent leg to do all the work. Perform exercise using both legs.

## Side-to-Side Box Shuffle

### Equipment:

A box 12 to 24 inches high.

### Start:

Stand to one side of the box with the left foot raised onto the middle of the box.

### Action:

Using a double arm swing, jump up and over to the other side of the box, landing with the right foot on top of the box and the left foot on the floor. This drill should be done in a continuous motion, shuffling back and forth across the top of the box.

## Front Box Jump

### Equipment:

A box (height 12 to 42 inches depending on ability).

### Start:

Stand facing the box with feet shoulder-width apart and hands behind the head.

### Action:

Jump up and land softly with both feet on the box. Step back down and repeat. For a more advanced exercise, hop down from the box and immediately jump back onto it. Use a variety of box heights, starting with 12-inch boxes, and building up to 42 inches with time.

## Lateral Box Jump

### Equipment:

A single box (or a row of 3 to 5 boxes) 12 to 42 inches high.

### Start:

Stand at the side of the box with feet shoulder-width apart.

### Action:

Jump onto the box and back to the ground on the other side. The exercise can be done as a single or as continuous movement across a line of 3 to 5 boxes of the same height (jumping to the ground between boxes).

# 30-, 60-, or 90-Second Box Drill

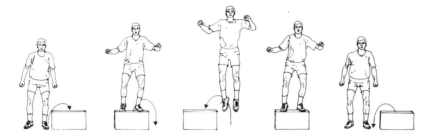

### Equipment:

A box 12 inches high, 20 inches wide, and 30 inches deep.

### Start:

Stand at the side of the box with feet shoulder-width apart.

### Action:

Jump onto the box, back to the ground on the other side, then back onto the box. Continue to jump across the top of the box for an allotted time, with each touch on top of the box counting as one. Use the following guidelines:

- 30 touches in 30 seconds—Start of training
- 60 touches in 60 seconds—Start of season
- 90 touches in 90 seconds—Championship season

# Multiple Box-to-Box Jumps

### Equipment:

Three to five boxes placed in a row (all the same height, dependent on ability).

### Start:

Stand with feet shoulder-width apart at the end of the row of boxes (with their length spread out before you).

### Action:

Jump onto the first box, then off on the other side, onto the second box, then off, and so on down the row. After jumping off the last box, walk back to the start (for recovery).

## Pyramiding Box Hops

### Equipment:
Three to five boxes of increasing height, evenly spaced 2 to 3 feet apart.

### Start:
Stand with feet shoulder-width apart at the end of the row of boxes.

### Action:
Jump onto the first box, then off on the other side, onto the second box, then off, and so on down the row. Walk back to the start after finishing the sequence (for recovery), or immediately hop back down the row of boxes.

## Multiple Box-to-Box Squat Jumps

### Equipment:
A row of boxes (all the same height, dependent on ability).

### Start:
Stand in a deep-squat position with feet shoulder-width apart at the end of the row of boxes.

### Action:
Jump to the first box, landing softly in a squat position. Maintaining the squat position, jump off the box on the other side and immediately onto and off of the following boxes. Keep hands on the hips or behind the head.

## Multiple Box-to-Box Jumps With Single Leg Landing

### Equipment:
A row of boxes 6 to 12 inches high. (Later increase height to 18 to 24 inches.)

### Start:
Stand on one foot at the end of the row of boxes.

### Action:
Jump onto the first box, landing on the takeoff foot, then jump to the floor, landing on the same foot. Continue in this fashion down the row of boxes. Repeat the exercise using the other leg. This is a strenuous exercise; the athlete must be in top form, and strict concentration is needed to prevent injury.

# DEPTH JUMPS

Jump From Box

Jump to Box

Step-Close Jump-and-Reach

Depth Jump

Depth Jump to Prescribed Height

Depth Jump to Rim Jump

Incline Push-Up Depth Jump

Squat Depth Jump

Depth Jump With 180-Degree Turn

Depth Jump With 360-Degree Turn

Single Leg Depth Jump

Depth Jump With Lateral Movement

Depth Jump With Stuff

Depth Jump With Blocking Bag

Depth Jump With Pass Catching

Depth Jump With Backward Glide

Handstand Depth Jump

Depth Jump Over Barrier

Depth Jump to Standing Long Jump

## Jump From Box

### Equipment:

A box 6 to 18 inches high.

### Start:

Stand on the box with feet shoulder-width apart.

### Action:

Squat slightly and step from the box and drop to the floor. Attempt to quickly absorb the landing and ''freeze'' as soon as contact is made with the ground.

## Jump to Box

### Equipment:

A box (6 to 12 inches high with a top surface no smaller than 24 inches square).

### Start:

Stand on the ground with feet shoulder-width apart, facing a box.

### Action:

Squat slightly and, using the double arm swing, jump from the ground onto the box.

## Step-Close Jump-and-Reach

### Equipment:

An object suspended at the peak of the athlete's jump.

### Start:

Stand in a staggered stance, front to back.

### Action:

Take a short step forward with the preferred foot and quickly bring the back foot together with the front foot (a step-close technique). Then jump vertically, reaching for the suspended object.

## Depth Jump

### Equipment:
A box 12 inches high.

### Start:
Stand on the box, toes close to the front edge.

### Action:
Step from the box and drop to land on both feet. Try to anticipate the landing and spring up as quickly as you can. Keep the body from "settling" on the landing, and make the ground contact as short as possible.

## Depth Jump to Prescribed Height

### Equipment:
Two boxes of equal height placed 2 to 4 feet apart (height and distance depend on ability).

### Start:
Stand on one box, toes close to the front edge and feet shoulder-width apart, facing the second box.

### Action:
Step off the box, landing on both feet, and jump onto the second box, landing lightly. The jump from the ground should be as quick as possible.

## Depth Jump to Rim Jump

### Equipment:
A box 12 to 42 inches high placed in front of an elevated marker (such as a basketball hoop).

### Start:
Stand on the box, toes close to the edge and facing the high object.

### Action:
Step off the box and land on both feet. Immediately jump up, reaching with one hand toward the marker, and then do repeated jumps, alternating hands and trying to reach the object each time. Time on the ground should be very short, with each jump being as high as the one before. Perform 3 to 5 rim jumps after each depth jump.

# Incline Push-Up Depth Jump

### Equipment:
Two mats, 3 to 4 inches high, placed shoulder-width apart, and a box high enough to elevate feet above the shoulders when the athlete is in a push-up position.

### Start:
Face the floor as if you were going to do a push-up, with your feet on the box and your hands between the mats.

### Action:
Push off the ground with your hands and land with one hand on each mat. Either remove one hand at a time from the mats and place it in the starting position, or for added difficulty, push off the mats with both hands and catch yourself in the starting position.

# Squat Depth Jump

### Equipment:
A box 12 to 42 inches high.

### Start:
Stand on a box in a quarter- to half-squat, toes close to the edge.

### Action:
Step off the box and land in a 90-degree squat position; explode up out of the squat and land solidly in a squat. For added difficulty, land on a second box of equal height after doing the jump.

# Depth Jump
# With 180-Degree Turn

### Equipment:
A box 12 to 42 inches high.

### Start:
Stand on a box, toes close to the edge.

### Action:
Step off the box and land on both feet. Immediately jump up and do a 180-degree turn in the air, landing again on both feet. For added difficulty, land on a second box after doing the turn.

## Depth Jump With 360-Degree Turn

**Equipment:**

A box 12 to 42 inches high.

**Start:**

Stand on a box, toes close to the edge.

**Action:**

Step off the box and land on both feet. Immediately jump up and do a 360-degree turn in the air, landing again on both feet. For added difficulty, land on a second box after doing the turn. This is a very advanced drill—it should not be performed by beginners.

## Single Leg Depth Jump

**Equipment:**

A box 12 to 18 inches high.

**Start:**

Stand on the box, toes close to the edge.

**Action:**

Step off the box and land on one foot. Then jump as high as possible, landing on the same foot. Keep the ground contact as short as possible. For added difficulty, jump to a second box after the jump. This is a very advanced drill; it should not be performed by beginners.

## Depth Jump With Lateral Movement

**Equipment:**

A partner and a box 12 to 42 inches high.

**Start:**

Stand on the box, toes close to the edge.

**Action:**

Step off the box and land on both feet. As you land, your partner points to the right or left; sprint in that direction for 10 to 12 meters.

## Depth Jump With Stuff

### Equipment:

A box 12 to 42 inches high, a basketball, and a basketball goal.

### Start:

Stand on the box, toes close to the edge, holding a ball in front of you.

### Action:

Step off the box and land on both feet. Explode up and forward while extending your arms and the ball up. Try to stuff the ball in the basket, or at least to touch the rim.

## Depth Jump With Blocking Bag

### Equipment:

A partner with a blocking bag, and a box 12 to 42 inches high.

### Start:

Stand on the box, toes close to the edge. The partner stands facing the box, about 4 feet away.

### Action:

Step off the box and land on both feet. Upon landing, explode into the blocking bag shoulder first.

## Depth Jump With Pass Catching

### Equipment:

A partner with a football, and a box 12 to 42 inches high.

### Start:

Stand on the box, toes close to the edge.

### Action:

Step off the box and land on both feet. Explode up and forward, extending your arms to catch a pass from your partner at the peak of your jump.

# Depth Jump With Backward Glide

### Equipment:
A box 12 to 42 inches high.

### Start:
Stand with heels close to the back of the box and with feet shoulder-width apart.

### Action:
Step backward off the box and land on both feet. Immediately upon landing, thrust one leg back and perform a glide pattern step as if shot putting.

# Handstand Depth Jump

### Equipment:
A partner and two mats or padded boxes, 3 to 4 inches high, placed shoulder-width apart.

### Start:
Stand between the mats or padded boxes, with a partner standing behind, and do a handstand on the floor.

### Action:
Push off the floor with the hands, landing with one hand on each mat. Then push up off the mats and land with your hands in their starting positions. The partner spots for athlete, ensuring that the body stays vertical.

# Depth Jump Over Barrier

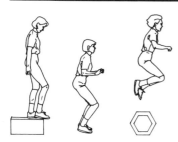

### Equipment:

A 12- to 42-inch box, and a barrier 28 to 36 inches high, placed about 3 feet from the box.

### Start:

Stand on the box with feet shoulder-width apart.

### Action:

Step off the box, and upon landing, jump over the barrier.

# Depth Jump to Standing Long Jump

### Equipment:

A box 12 to 42 inches high.

### Start:

Stand on the box, feet shoulder-width apart and toes close to the edge.

### Action:

Step off the box and land on both feet. Immediately upon landing, jump as far forward as possible, again landing on both feet.

# BOUNDING

Skipping

Power Skipping

Side Skipping With Big Arm Swing

Backward Skipping

Moving Split Squat With Cycle

Alternate Bounding With Single Arm Action

Alternate Bounding With Double Arm Action

Combination Bounding With Single Arm Action

Combination Bounding With Double Arm Action

Combination Bounding With Vertical Jump

Single Leg Bounding

# Skipping

### Equipment:
None.

### Start:
Stand comfortably.

### Action:
Lift the right leg with the knee bent 90 degrees while lifting the left arm, with the elbows also bent 90 degrees. As these two limbs come back down, lift the opposite limbs with the same motion. For added difficulty, push off the ground for more upward extention.

# Power Skipping

### Equipment:
None.

### Start:
Stand comfortably.

### Action:
Hold both arms out in front of you at shoulder height. Move forward in a skipping motion and bring the lead foot up to attempt to touch the hands. Repeat the motion with the opposite leg and continue skipping for the prescribed distance.

# Side Skipping With Big Arm Swing

### Equipment:

None.

### Start:

Stand with feet together.

### Action:

This exercise looks like a jumping jack: Slide step to the side, swinging the arms up and over the head. As you push to bring the feet back together, the arms come back down and cross in front of the body. Keep performing this extended side step and arm swing for a prescribed distance (about 40 to 50 meters).

# Backward Skipping

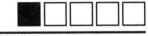

### Equipment:

A mark 20 to 30 meters from the start.

### Start:

Stand on one foot.

### Action:

Skip backward for 20 to 30 meters. Coordinate the arm swing with the skip to add to the backward propulsion.

# Moving Split Squat With Cycle

### Equipment:
A 30-meter mark.

### Start:
Spread the feet apart, front to back, and bend the front leg 90 degrees.

### Action:
Jumping up and forward, switch legs. As you bring the back leg through, try to touch the buttock. Land in the split-squat position and immediately do another cycle, continuing for a prescribed distance (about 30 meters). Each push from the ground has to propel the body forward. This is an advanced drill.

# Alternate Bounding With Single Arm Action

### Equipment:
None.

### Start:
Jog into the start of the drill to increase forward momentum. As you jog, start the drill with the right foot forward and the left foot back.

### Action:
This drill is simply an exaggerated running action. Push off with the left foot and bring the leg forward, with the knee bent and the thigh parallel to the ground. At the same time reach forward with the right arm. As the left leg comes through, the right leg extends back and remains extended for the duration of the push-off. Hold this extended stride for a brief time, then land on the left foot. The right leg then drives through to the front bent position, the left arm reaches forward, and the left leg extends back. Make each stride long, and try to cover as much distance as possible.

# Alternate Bounding With Double Arm Action

### Equipment:
None.

### Start:
Jog into the start of the drill to increase forward momentum. As you jog, start the drill with the right foot forward and the left foot back.

### Action:
Push off with the left foot and bring the leg forward, with the knee bent and the thigh parallel to the ground. At the same time bring both arms forward with great force to help propel the body forward. As the left leg comes through, the right leg extends back and remains extended for the duration of the push-off. Hold this extended stride for a brief time, quickly bring both arms behind the body, then land on the left foot. The right leg then drives through to the front bent position, the arms come forward, the left leg extends back, and the arms move back. This drill is an exaggerated running action; make each stride long, and try to cover as much distance as possible.

# Combination Bounding With Single Arm Action

### Equipment:
None.

### Start:
Stand on one foot.

### Action:
In combination bounding you bound on one foot in a set sequence: right-right-left, or left-left-right. Bound from one foot, then the same foot, then the other foot. The right arm moves forward with the left foot, and vice versa. Continue bounding by repeating the cycle.

## Combination Bounding With Double Arm Action

### Equipment:
None.

### Start:
Stand on one foot.

### Action:
In combination bounding you bound on one foot in a set sequence: right-right-left, or left-left-right. Bound from one foot, then the same foot, then the other foot. Swing both arms forward on each bound, very quickly, to keep the body balanced and the motion of the bound smooth.

## Combination Bounding With Vertical Jump

### Equipment:
None.

### Start:
Stand on one foot.

### Action:
Do a combination bounding sequence (right-right-left or left-left-right), then follow immediately with a strong vertical jump. On the third bound, bring the nonbounding foot up to meet the bounding foot so that the jump is off both feet. Use a double arm swing to assist in lifting you vertically. As soon as you land from the vertical jump, complete another bounding sequence.

# Single Leg Bounding

## Equipment:
None.

## Start:
Stand on one foot.

## Action:
Bound from one foot as far forward as possible, using the other leg and arms to cycle in the air for balance and to increase forward momentum. Advanced athletes should try to touch the heel of the bounding foot to the buttocks with each bound. Continue bounding for a prescribed distance (about 40 meters). This drill should be performed on both legs for equal strength.

# MEDICINE BALL EXERCISES

Front Toss

Heel Toss

Over-Under

Trunk Rotation

Underhand Throw

Pullover Pass

Side Throw

Overhead Throw

Low Post Drill

Backward Throw

Backward Throw With Jump to Box

Kneeling Side Throw

Power Drop

Catch and Pass With Jump-and-Reach

## Front Toss

### Equipment:
A medicine ball.

### Start:
Stand with the ball held between your feet.

### Action:
Jump up with the ball, then toss it to yourself while in the air. After catching it, drop the ball to the ground between your feet and repeat.

## Heel Toss

### Equipment:
A medicine ball.

### Start:
Stand with the ball held between your heels.

### Action:
Use the heel of one foot to flick the ball up and over your back and shoulders, and catch it in front of your body. This toss requires a quick flexion of the knee and considerable effort from the hamstring muscles.

## Over-Under

### Equipment:
A medicine ball.

### Start:
Sit on the floor with your legs straight in front of you.

### Action:
Lift your right leg and pass the ball under it from the inside. Then pass it over the top of your right leg, under your left leg from the inside, and over the top of your left leg (so the ball makes a figure eight around your legs).

## Trunk Rotation

### Equipment:
A medicine ball.

### Start:
Sit on the floor with your legs spread and the ball behind your back.

### Action:
Rotate to the right, pick up the ball, bring it around to your left side, and replace it behind your back (so the ball makes a circle around your body). Repeat for the prescribed repetitions and then reverse directions.

## Underhand Throw

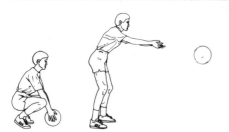

### Equipment:

A partner and a medicine ball.

### Start:

Stand in a squat about 3 meters from your partner holding the ball close to the ground.

### Action:

Keeping your back straight, raise straight up and throw the ball up and out to your partner, using the legs to provide momentum.

## Pullover Pass

### Equipment:

A partner and a medicine ball.

### Start:

Lie on your back with your knees bent, holding the ball over your head, while your partner stands at your feet.

### Action:

Keeping your arms extended, pass the ball to your partner. Your partner can back up to require you to throw farther for increased intensity.

## Side Throw

### Equipment:

A medicine ball and a partner or large solid barrier.

### Start:

Holding a medicine ball on your right, stand with feet shoulder-width apart.

### Action:

Swing the ball farther to the right and then forcefully reverse directions to the left and release. You may toss the ball to a partner or throw it against a solid barrier (e.g., a gym wall).

## Overhead Throw

### Equipment:
A medicine ball and a partner.

### Start:
Stand with a medicine ball overhead.

### Action:
Step forward and bring the ball sharply forward with both arms throwing it to a partner, or over a specific distance.

## Low Post Drill

### Equipment:
A partner, a medicine ball, and a basketball goal.

### Start:
Stand with your back to the basket, about a meter to the front or side.

### Action:
Your partner starts the drill by throwing you the ball in the low post position. Catch it, pivot, and jump to touch the ball against the rim. Immediately after landing, jump to touch the rim with the ball a second time. Finally, pivot back toward your partner and pass the ball to him or her.

## Backward Throw

### Equipment:

A partner and a medicine ball.

### Start:

Stand about 3 meters in front of your partner, facing the same direction and holding the ball in front of you.

### Action:

Holding the ball between your legs, squat down and then toss the ball up and over your head to your partner. Be careful to bend your knees, bend from your hips, and keep your back straight.

## Backward Throw With Jump to Box

### Equipment:

A box 12 to 42 inches high and a medicine ball.

### Start:

Squat facing the box and holding a medicine ball.

### Action:

Lower the ball between your legs, then toss it up and back over your head. As you thrust upward to toss the ball, push off the ground and land on the box. Step off the box and collect the ball for the next repetition.

## Kneeling Side Throw

### Equipment:

A partner and a medicine ball.

### Start:

Kneel facing your partner, about 3 meters away, and hold the ball to one side with both hands at the level of your hip.

### Action:

Twist your upper body and arms together and throw the ball to your partner.

# Power Drop

### Equipment:

A partner, a box 12 to 42 inches high, and a medicine ball.

### Start:

Lie supine on the ground with arms outstretched. Partner stands on the box holding the medicine ball at arms length.

### Action:

Partner drops the ball. Catch the ball and immediately propel the ball back to the partner. Repeat.

# Catch and Pass With Jump-and-Reach

### Equipment:

A partner, a box 12 to 42 inches high, a medicine ball, and a high object (like a basketball goal).

### Start:

Stand on the box, feet shoulder-width apart and toes close to the edge.

### Action:

Step off the box and land on both feet. Explode up and forward, extend your arms, and catch a pass from your partner. Upon landing, explode up again and reach for the high object with the medicine ball.

# CHAPTER 5
# SPORT-SPECIFIC DRILLS

This chapter shows you five plyometric exercises that are most beneficial for each of 19 different sports or activities. An illustrated sequence of the exercise technique is shown, along with the name of the exercise and the page number on which the full explanation appears in chapter 4.

# Baseball and Softball

 Side Throw (p. 64)

 Overhead Throw (p. 65)

 Lateral Jump With Two Feet (p. 32)

 Standing Long Jump (p. 31)

Alternate Bounding With Single Arm Action (p. 58)

# Basketball

 Rim Jumps (p. 38)

 Low Post Drill (p. 65)

 Depth Jump With Stuff (p. 52)

 Lateral Cone Hops (p. 39)

 Depth Jump With 180-Degree Turn (p. 50)

# Bicycling

Split Squat With Cycle (p. 29)

Single Leg Push-Off (p. 43)

Alternating Push-Off (p. 43)

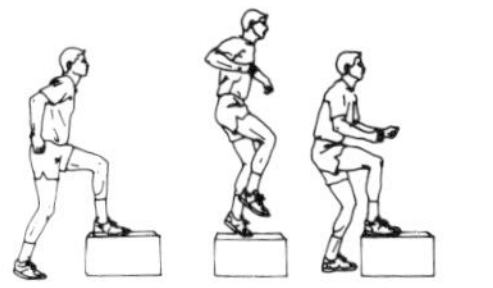

Squat Depth Jump (p. 50)

Stadium Hops (p. 40)

# Diving

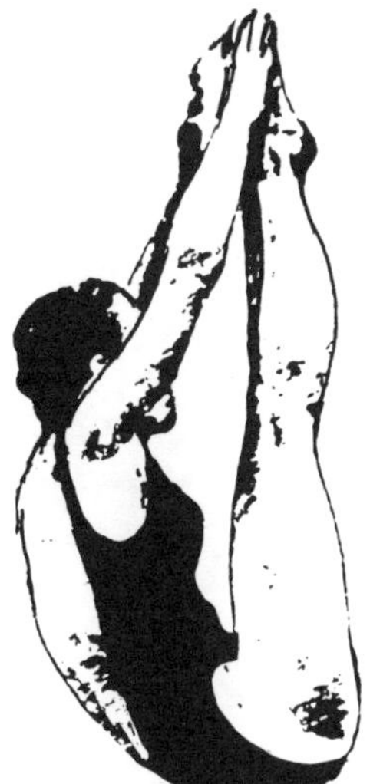

Alternating Push-Off (p. 43)

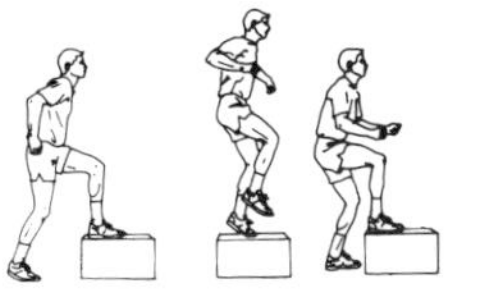

Straight Pike Jump (p. 29)

Front Box Jump (p. 44)

Step-Close Jump-and-Reach (p. 48)

Depth Jump Over Barrier (p. 54)

# Downhill Skiing

Stadium Hops (p. 40)

Zig-Zag Drill (p. 41)

Hip-Twist Ankle Hop (p. 27)

90-Second Box Drill (p. 45)

Diagonal Cone Hops (p. 37)

# Figure Skating

Split Pike Jump (p. 29)

Depth Jump With
180-Degree Turn (p. 50)

Split Squat With Cycle (p. 29)

Straddle Jump
to Camel Landing (p. 33)

Double Leg Hops (p. 39)

Double Leg Hops (p. 39)

**Football**

Standing Long Jump
With Lateral Sprint (p. 33)

Depth Jump With
Blocking Bag (p. 52)

Depth Jump With
Pass Catching (p. 52)

90-Second Box Drill (p. 45)

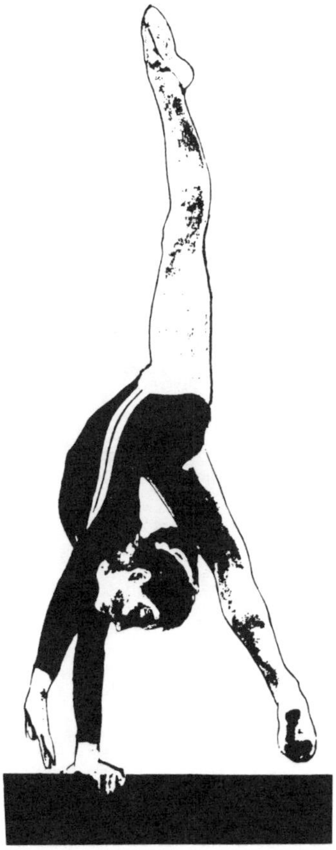

Handstand Depth Jump (p.
53)

**Gymnastics**

Incline Push-Up Depth Jump
(p. 50)

Depth Jump From
12-Inch Height (p. 49)

Split Pike Jump (p. 29)

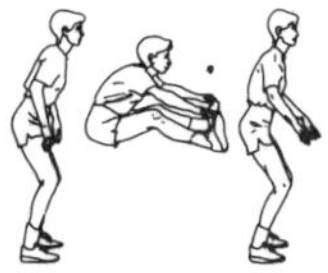

Pyramiding Box Hops (p. 46)

# Ice Hockey

 Split Squat With Cycle (p. 29)

 Lateral Cone Hops (p. 39)

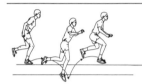 Lateral Jump With Single Leg (p. 33)

 90-Second Box Drill (p. 45)

 Zig-Zag Drill (p. 41)

# Soccer

 Split Squat Jump (p. 28)

 Lateral Jump Over Barrier (p. 34)

 Alternating Push-Off (p. 43)

 Cone Hops With 180-Degree Turn (p. 38)

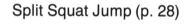 Overhead Throw (p. 65)

# Swimming

Standing Long Jump (p. 31)

Double Leg Hops (p. 39)

Overhead Throw (p. 65)

Depth Jump to Standing Long Jump (p. 54)

Backward Throw (p. 66)

# Tennis

Lateral Cone Hops (p. 39)

Side-to-Side Box Shuffle (p. 44)

Cone Hops With Change-of-Direction Sprint (p. 38)

Single Leg Push-Off (p. 43)

Depth Jump With Lateral Movement (p. 51)

# Track and Field: Jumping Events

 Stadium Hops (p. 40)

 Alternate Bounding With Double Arm Action (p. 59)

 Combination Bounding With Double Arm Action (p. 60)

 Single Leg Bounding (p. 61)

 1-2-3 Drill (p. 32)

# Track and Field: Sprints

 Barrier Hops (Hurdle Hops) (p. 40)

 Standing Long Jump (p. 31)

 Standing Triple Jump (p. 35)

 Alternate Bounding With Double Arm Action (p. 59)

 Double Leg Hops (p. 39)

Backward Skipping (p. 57)

Backward Throw With
Jump to Box (p. 66)

Depth Jump With
180-Degree Turn (p. 50)

Depth Jump With
Backward Glide (p. 53)

Power Drop (p. 67)

# Track and Field:
# Throwing Events

Multiple Box-to-Box
Squat Jumps (p. 46)

Depth Jump (p. 49)

90-Second Box Drill (p. 45)

Split Squat Jump (p. 28)

Rim Jumps (p. 38)

# Volleyball

# Weight Lifting

| | |
|---|---|
| | Split Squat Jump (p. 29) |
| | Multiple Box-to-Box Squat Jumps (p. 46) |
| | Stadium Hops (p. 40) |
| | Depth Jump (p. 49) |
| | Rim Jumps (p. 38) |

# Wrestling

| | |
|---|---|
| | Stadium Hops (p. 40) |
| | Moving Split Squat With Cycle (p. 58) |
| | Zig-Zag Drill (p. 41) |
| | Multiple Box-to-Box Squat Jumps (p. 46) |
| | Lateral Cone Hops (p. 39) |

# BIBLIOGRAPHY

Adams, T. (1984). An investigation of selected plyometric training exercises on muscular leg strength and power. *Track and Field Quarterly Review*, **84**(1), 36-40.

Asmussen, E., & Bonde-Peterson, F. (1974). Storage of elastic energy in skeletal muscles in man. *Acta Physiologica Scandinavica*, **91**, 385-392.

Auferoth, S.J. (1986). Power training for the developing thrower. *National Strength Coaches Association Journal*, **8**(5), 56-62.

Bielik, E., Chu, D., & Costello, F., et al. (1986). Roundtable: Practical considerations for utilizing plyometrics, part 1. *National Strength Coaches Association Journal*, **8**(3), 14-22.

Bielik, E., Chu, D., & Costello, F., et al. (1986). Roundtable: Practical considerations for utilizing plyometrics, part 2. *National Strength Coaches Association Journal*, **8**(4), 14-24.

Blattner, S., & Noble, L. (1979). Relative effects of isokinetic and plyometric training on vertical jumping performance. *Research Quarterly*, **50**(4), 583-588.

Bosco, C. (1982). Physiological considerations on vertical jump exercise after drops from variable heights. *Volleyball Technical Journal*, **6**, 53-58.

Bosco, C., & Komi, P. (1979). Potentiation of the mechanical behavior of the human skeletal muscle through prestretching. *Acta Physiologica Scandinavica*, **106**, 467-472.

Bosco, C., Komi, P.V., Pulli, P., Pittera, C., & Montoneu, J. (1982). Considerations of the training of the elastic potential of the human skeletal muscle. *Volleyball Technical Journal*, **6**, 75-81.

Bosco, C., Luhtanen, P., & Komi, P. (1976). Kinetics and kinematics of the takeoff in the long jump. In P. Komi (Ed.), *Biomechanics VB* (pp. 174-180). Baltimore: University Park Press.

Brant, J. (1988, September). I'd like to explode. *Outside Magazine*, pp. 29-31.

Brown, M.E., Mayhew, J.L., & Boleach, L.W. (1986). The effect of plyometric training on the vertical jump of high school boys' basketball players. *Journal of Sports Medicine and Physical Fitness*, **26**(1), 1-4.

Cavagna, G. (1970). Elastic bounce of the body. *Journal of Applied Physiology*, **29**(3), 279-282.

Chu, D. (1983). Plyometrics: The link between strength and speed. *National Strength Coaches Association Journal*, **5**(2), 20-21.

Chu, D. (1984). The language of plyometrics. *National Strength Coaches Association Journal*, **6**(4), 30-31.

Chu, D. (1984). Plyometric exercise. *National Strength Coaches Association Journal*, **6**(5), 56-62.

Chu, D. (1989). *Plyometric exercises with the medicine ball*. Liverpool, CA: Bittersweet.

Costello, F. (1984). *Bounding to the Top*. Los Altos, CA: Tafnew.

Drez, D., Paine, R., & Roberts, T. (1987). *Abstract: Functional testing of 50 high school football players*. Unpublished study.

Duda, M. (1988). Plyometrics: A legitimate form of power training? *The Physician and Sportsmedicine Journal*, **16**(3), 218.

Dursenev, L., & Raeysky, L. (1979). Strength training for jumpers. *Soviet Sports Review*, **14**(2), 53-55.

Dyatchkov, V.M. (1969). High jumping, track technique. *Journal of Technical Track and Field Athletics*, **36**, 1123-1158.

Gambetta, V. (1978). Plyometric training. *USTCA Quarterly Review*, **2**, 58-59.

Grieve, D.W. (1970). Stretching active muscles. *Track Technique*, **42**, 1333-1335.

Huber, J. (1987). Increasing a diver's vertical jump through plyometric training. *National Strength Coaches Association Journal*, **9**(1), 34-36.

Komi, P.V. (1979). Neuromuscular performance: Factors influencing force and speed production. *Scandinavian Journal of Sports Science*, **1**, 2-15.

Komi, P.V., & Bosco, C. (1978). Utilization of stored elastic energy in leg extensor muscles by men and women. *Medicine and Science in Sports and Exercise*, **10**(4), 261-265.

Komi, P.V, & Buskirk, E. (1972). Effect of eccentric and concentric muscle conditioning on tension and electrical activity of human muscle. *Ergonomics*, **15**, 417-434.

Lundin, P. (1985). A review of plyometric training. *National Strength Coaches Association Journal*, **7**(69), 69-74.

Matveyey, L. (1977). *Fundamentals of Sports Training*. Moscow: Progress Publishers.

McFarlane, B. (1983). Special strength: Horizontal

and/or vertical? *Track and Field Quarterly Review*, **83**(4), 51-53.

Miller, J. (1981). Plyometric training for speed. *National Strength Coaches Association Journal*, **2**(3), 20-22.

Plisk, S. (1988). Physiological training for competitive alpine skiing. *National Strength Coaches Association Journal*, **10**(1), 30-33.

Polhemus, R.W. (1980). The effects of plyometric training with ankle and vest weights on conventional weight programs for men. *Texas Coach*, 16-17.

Polhemus, R.W. (1980, February). The effects of plyometric training with ankle and vest weights on conventional weight programs for women. *Texas Coach*, 16-18.

Polhemus, R.W., & Burkhardt, E. (1980, March). The effects of plyometric training drills on the physical strength gains of collegiate football players. *National Strength Coaches Association Journal*, **2**(1), 13-15.

Rasulbekov, R.A., Fomin, R.A., Chulkov, V.U., & Chudovsky, V.I. (1986). Does a swimmer need explosive strength? *National Strength Coaches Association Journal*, **8**(2), 56-57.

Scoles, G. (1978). Depth jumping! Does it really work? *Athletic Journal*, **58**, 48-75.

Stone, M.H., & O'Bryant, H.S. (1987). *Weight training: A scientific approach*. Edina, MN: Burgess International Group.

Vermeil, A. (1989). Game day inseason training for the Chicago Bulls. *National Strength Coaches Association Journal*, **11**(1), 47-48.

Vermeil, A., & Chu, D. (1982). Periodization of strength training for professional football. *National Strength Coaches Association Journal*, **4**(3), 54-55

Vermeil, A., & Chu, D. (1983). A theoretical approach to planning a football season. *National Strength Coaches Association Journal*, **4**(6), 33-36.

Verhoshanski, V. (1967). Are depth jumps useful? *Track and Field*, **12**, 9.

Verhoshanski, V. (1969). Perspectives in the improvement of speed-strength preparation of jumpers. *Review of Soviet Physical Education and Sports*, **4**(2), 28-29.

Verhoshanski, V., & Chernovsov, G. (1974). Jumps in the training of a sprinter. *Track and Field*, **9**, 16-17.

Verhoshanski, V., & Tatyan, V. (1983). Speed-strength preparation of future champions. *Soviet Sports Review*, **18**(4), 166-170.

Wilt, F. (1975). Plyometrics—What it is and how it works. *Athletic Journal*, **55**(5), 76, 89-90.

Worlick, M. (1983). Power development through plyometric exercise. *Soccer Journal*, **27**, 39-41.

Yessis, M. (1982). Soviet conditioning for American football. *National Strength Coaches Association Journal*, **4**(1), 4-7.